Cash Flow Freedom

Cynthia DeLuca

Copyright © 2026 by Cynthia M. DeLuca

www.CynthiaDeLuca.com

Print ISBN: 979-8-9953528-0-8

Also by Cynthia DeLuca

The High Heels Landlord:

A step-by-step guide for women for successful real estate investing

Fill'er Up!:

The High Heels Landlord's Guide to Filling Your Rental Property

The Standout Agent:

How to stand out from the competition and experience higher success in your real estate career

A Note on the Use of Artificial Intelligence

This book was written by a real estate investor and educator with decades of hands-on experience in the field. Artificial intelligence tools were used solely as a support resource in the creation of this work, assisting with brainstorming, grammar, formatting, and editorial refinement.

Every concept, strategy, story, and lesson within these pages reflects the author's real-life journey, personal experiences, and professional expertise. AI did not generate the ideas, opinions, or guidance found in this book. It served as a tool, not a voice.

The wisdom here is earned, not artificial.

Dedication

This book is dedicated to my husband, business
partner, and soul mate.

We did it. We achieved cash flow freedom.

INTRODUCTION

INTRODUCTION

Why Rental Properties Are Your Path to Cash Flow Freedom

Let me ask you a question: When was the last time you woke up on a Tuesday morning and decided you didn't feel like working that day, and actually didn't?

If you're like most people, the answer is never. You show up. You clock in. You trade hours for dollars, whether you're working for someone else or running your own business. And somewhere in the back of your mind, there's a nagging question: When does this end?

Here's the uncomfortable truth: If you stopped working today, how long could you maintain your current lifestyle? A month? Six months? Maybe a year if you've been diligent with savings?

That's not freedom. That's a treadmill with a nicer view.

The Problem with Traditional Retirement Planning

We've all been sold the same story: Work for 40 years, save 10–15% of your income, put it in a 401(k), hope the market cooperates, and maybe, *maybe*, you can retire at 65 with enough money to not be a burden to your kids.

That's not a plan. That's a prayer.

And even if it works, you've spent the best years of your life, your energy, your health, your time with your family, building someone else's dream while postponing your own. There has to be a better way.

The Solution: Cash Flow Freedom

There is a better way, and it's been hiding in plain sight for generations: rental real estate.

This book is about achieving cash flow freedom, the point where passive income from your properties covers your living expenses, and you never have to work for money again. Not "financial independence." Not "building wealth." *Cash flow freedom.*

Here's what makes it different: While you're sleeping, eating dinner with your family, or taking a vacation, rental properties are creating cash flow through four powerful forces.

1. **Cash Flow.** Tenants pay you every month, creating income without you trading time for it.

2. **Appreciation.** Your properties grow in value over time.

3. **Mortgage Paydown.** Your tenants pay down your loan, building equity automatically.

4. **Tax Advantages.** The government incentivizes real estate investment, letting you keep more of what you earn.

These four forces don't work separately, they compound together, creating wealth that builds momentum over time. But the foundation of everything is cash flow. Without cash flow, none of the other pillars matter.

Who This Book Is For

This book is for you if you are tired of trading time for money with no end in sight, and you want cash flow freedom: the ability to retire early or at least have the option. It is for you if you are willing to learn and take action without quitting your day job to "get into real estate," and if you want passive income that supports your life rather than just another job. Most importantly, it is for you if you are looking for a proven path, not a get-rich-quick scheme.

This book is NOT for you if you are looking for ways to flip houses, wholesale deals, or become a real estate guru on social media. Those strategies might make you money, but they will not buy you cash flow freedom. They are simply another job.

What You'll Learn

By the time you finish this book, you will know exactly how much monthly cash flow you need for freedom, and it is probably less than you think. You will learn how to find, analyze, and purchase your first cash-flowing property, even if you believe you do not have enough money to start. You will understand the difference between looking wealthy and having cash flow freedom, and why most investors are chasing the wrong goal. You will know how to build a portfolio that generates enough cash flow to replace your income, and you will have the systems to manage your properties without letting them steal back your freedom.

Your Cash Flow Freedom Starts Now

I'm not going to promise you'll be free in six months or that you'll own 100 properties in five years. What I will tell you is this: If you follow the blueprint in this book, you'll be on a clear path to cash flow freedom, whether that's in 5 years, 10 years, or 15 years.

The question isn't whether this works. Thousands of people have already achieved cash flow freedom through rental real estate, including me. The question is whether you're ready to start.

Let's build your cash flow freedom.

PART 1:

THE CASH FLOW FOUNDATION

Chapter 1: The Four Pillars of Rental Property Wealth

Most people think real estate investing is about buying low and selling high. While that may sound like a good plan, that's speculation, not investment. Real wealth in rental real estate, the kind that leads to cash flow freedom, comes from holding properties long-term and letting four powerful forces build your wealth simultaneously.

Let's break down each pillar.

Pillar 1: Cash Flow. The Foundation of Your Freedom.

Cash flow is the lifeblood of your rental property business and the direct path to freedom. It is the money left over after all expenses are paid, including mortgage, taxes, insurance, maintenance, property management, and reserves.

Here is a simple example:

Monthly Rent Collected:	**$2,000**
Mortgage Payment:	$1,200
Property Taxes:	$200
Insurance:	$130
Property Management (10%):	$200
Maintenance Reserve:	$120
Total Expenses:	$1,850
Monthly Cash Flow:	**$150**

That $150 might not sound like much, but here's what makes it powerful.

1. **It is passive.** You are not trading hours for it.

2. **It is consistent.** It comes in whether you work that month or not.

3. **It scales.** Ten properties producing $150 per month equals $1,500 per month, or $18,000 per year, without working.

4. **It is freedom.** Enough cash flow means you never have to work again.

Cash flow is the difference between owning real estate and owning a time-sucking money pit. Every property you buy must produce positive cash flow from day one, or it does not belong in your portfolio.

Without cash flow, you have no path to freedom. That is why it is Pillar #1.

Pillar 2: Appreciation. Your Property Growing in Value.

While your tenants are paying you monthly cash flow, your property is typically increasing in value over time.

Historically, real estate appreciates at roughly 3 to 4% annually, though this varies by market. Using a conservative 3% example with a purchase price of $285,000:

Purchase Price: **$285,000**

Year 1 Appreciation (3%): $8,550

Year 5 Appreciation: $45,393

Year 10 Appreciation: $98,017

Year 20 Appreciation: $229,742

Your $285,000 property is now worth $514,742, and you didn't do anything except hold it.

But here's the kicker: That appreciation is happening on the entire property value, not just your down payment. If you put $57,000 down (20%), you are getting appreciation on $285,000 worth of real estate. That is leverage working in your favor.

There are two types of appreciation.

1. **Natural Appreciation.** The market goes up over time due to inflation, demand, and limited supply.

2. **Forced Appreciation.** You increase the value through renovations, adding features or more square footage, or improving the property.

Both matter, but natural appreciation is what happens while you sleep. Forced appreciation is a bonus when you buy right.

Appreciation builds your net worth, but cash flow builds your freedom. Never sacrifice cash flow for appreciation potential.

Pillar 3: Mortgage Paydown. Tenants Buying the Property for You.

This is the pillar most new investors overlook, and it is one of the most powerful.

Every month, your tenant's rent payment includes a portion that pays down your mortgage principal. In the early years it is small, but over time it accelerates.

With a $285,000 property, a $228,000 mortgage at 7 percent interest over 30 years:

> Year 1 Principal Paydown: ~$2,100/year
>
> Year 5 Principal Paydown: ~$3,200/year
>
> Year 10 Principal Paydown: ~$4,600/year
>
> Year 20 Principal Paydown: ~$9,300/year

By year 10, the tenant is paying down nearly $5,000 a year of your principal debt, on top of your monthly cash flow to your pocket. Over 30 years, your tenants will have paid off the entire $228,000 loan for you.

Think about that: You put $57,000 down, and 30 years later you own a property worth $514,000 or more, and you did not pay the mortgage. Your tenants did.

As time goes on, your rents increase, cash flow increases. You can make extra principal payments to cut the 30 years of debt down to 20, or maybe even 15.

Once mortgages start paying off, your cash flow per property explodes. A property cash flowing $300 per month with a mortgage might cash flow $1,100 to $2,000 per month once paid off. That is when cash flow freedom accelerates dramatically.

Pillar 4: Tax Advantages. Keeping More of What You Earn.

The U.S. tax code is written to incentivize real estate investment. Here is how it works in your favor.

Depreciation.

The IRS allows you to depreciate your residential rental property over 27.5 years, even though it is likely appreciating in value. This creates a paper loss that offsets your rental income.

Property Value:	$285,000
Land Value (est.):	$57,000
Building Value:	$228,000
Annual Depreciation:	$228,000 ÷ 27.5 = $8,291/year

If your property cash flows $1,800 per year ($150 per month), you can deduct $8,291 in depreciation, showing a $6,491 loss on paper, even though you pocketed $1,800 in real cash. That paper loss can offset other income.

Other tax benefits include:

- Mortgage interest is deductible.
- Property expenses such as repairs, management, and travel to the property are deductible.
- 1031 exchanges allow you to defer capital gains taxes when selling.
- Long-term capital gains rates, which are lower than ordinary income rates, apply when you do sell.

Consult a CPA who understands real estate. The tax advantages are real and significant, and they help you keep more of your cash flow, getting you to freedom faster.

The Compounding Effect

Here is where it all comes together. These four pillars do not work in isolation...they compound.

Revisiting our $285,000 property in Year 1:

- **$1,800 cash flow** plus **$8,550 appreciation** plus **$2,100 mortgage paydown** equals $12,450 total wealth increase, plus tax savings.

Your $57,000 down payment just earned you approximately a 22 percent return.

Try getting that from a savings account.

Now imagine five properties. Ten properties. Twenty properties.

That is how you achieve cash flow freedom. That is how you retire early. That is how you own your time.

Chapter 2: Rich vs. Affluent vs. Wealthy. Why Cash Flow Freedom Matters.

Walk into any real estate investor meetup and you'll hear the same bragging:

> **"I've got 47 doors."**
>
> **"I just closed on my 12th property this year."**
>
> **"My portfolio is worth $4.2 million."**

And while everyone is nodding and impressed, here is the question nobody is asking:

> **"How much cash flow do you actually take home every month?"**

Crickets.

Because here is the dirty secret of real estate investing. Most people are confusing activity with achievement. They are chasing numbers that look good on paper but do not create actual cash flow freedom.

Let me introduce you to three people. They all invest in real estate, but their lives look very different.

Meet Rich Robert

Robert is a successful surgeon making $400,000 a year.
He drives a Tesla, lives in a beautiful home, and his kids go
to private school. By most standards, Robert is doing great.

But here is Robert's problem: If he stops working, the
money stops. All of it.

Robert is rich. He has a high income. But he is still trading
time for money. He is one bad diagnosis, one malpractice
suit, or one burnout away from his entire lifestyle
collapsing.

Robert has zero cash flow freedom. High income does not
equal freedom. It just means you have a nicer cage.

Meet Affluent Angela

Angela looks wealthy. She owns 22 rental properties worth
$3.8 million. She drives a Range Rover with a vanity plate
that says "RENTAL QUEEN." Her Instagram is full of
closing photos and property tours.

But here is what Angela does not post:

- Her properties are barely breaking even because
  she overpaid in a hot market.

- She is covering negative cash flow out of pocket on
  four of them.

- She spends 30 hours a week managing tenants,
  contractors, and problems.

- She cannot take a vacation because something
  always breaks.

- She is stressed, exhausted, and one major repair
  away from a financial crisis.

Angela is affluent. She looks wealthy and has a large portfolio. But she has created another job for herself, not freedom. She is a slave to her properties.

Angela has negative cash flow freedom. She is asset-rich but cash-poor, working harder than ever.

Meet Wealthy William

William owns seven rental properties. His portfolio is worth $1.4 million, which is nothing flashy. But here is what matters:

- Each property cash flows $300 to $500 per month after all expenses.

- Total monthly cash flow: $2,800.

- Annual cash flow: $33,600.

- He uses a property manager, so his time investment is about two hours per month.

William's properties cover his mortgage, his car payment, his groceries, and his insurance. He still works, but he does not have to. And in five years, when two more mortgages are paid off, his cash flow will double.

William has achieved cash flow freedom. He has assets that produce income without requiring his time. He owns his life.

The Critical Difference

Let's break this down.

Rich means high income. You make a lot of money, but you trade time for it. Stop working and the money stops. Cash flow freedom: 0 percent.

Affluent means high net worth. You own a lot of assets on paper, but they do not produce enough cash flow to support your life. You are asset-rich and cash-poor. Cash flow freedom: 0 percent.

Wealthy means cash flow freedom. You own assets that generate income without requiring your time. You can stop working and maintain your lifestyle. Cash flow freedom: 100 percent.

The goal of this book is not to make you rich or affluent. The goal is to give you cash flow freedom.

The Trap of Counting Doors

Here is where most investors go wrong: They think the goal is to own as many properties as possible.

"I want 10 doors by next year."

"I'm trying to get to 50 units."

"My goal is 100 doors."

This is ego-driven investing, and it is a trap. Let me show you why.

Scenario A: 10 Properties.

- Average cash flow per property: $200 per month.
- Total monthly cash flow: $2,000.
- Time to cash flow freedom: Longer.

Scenario B: 4 Properties.

- Average cash flow per property: $600 per month.
- Total monthly cash flow: $2,400.
- Time to cash flow freedom: Faster.

Scenario B has fewer properties, less headache, less management, and more cash flow freedom. Which investor is better off? The one with four properties, every single time.

Cash Flow Is Freedom. Units Are Just Tools.

Here is the mindset shift you need to make. Stop asking how many doors you have. Start asking how much cash flow you are generating toward your freedom number.

A single fourplex producing $800 per month gets you closer to cash flow freedom than four single-family homes producing $150 per month each. A duplex cash flowing $500 per month beats a fancy Airbnb that is vacant half the time.

The metric that matters is this:

Monthly cash flow ÷ Your monthly expenses = Your freedom percentage

If your monthly expenses are $4,000 and your properties produce $4,000 per month in cash flow, you are at 100 percent cash flow freedom. You can work if you want to, but you do not have to.

That is the goal. Not 100 doors. Not a $10 million portfolio.
Cash flow that covers your life.

Why Cash Flow Freedom Matters

The real estate world is full of people who look successful
but are drowning in stress, negative cash flow, and time
commitments. They bought properties to impress other
investors, not to build cash flow freedom.

Do not be that person.

Build for cash flow. Build for freedom. Build a portfolio
that serves your life, not one that consumes it.

*In the next chapter, we are going to figure out exactly how
much cash flow you need for freedom, and how many
properties it will take to get there.*

Chapter 3: Your Cash Flow Freedom Number

Let's get specific. No more vague goals like "I want to be financially free someday." We are going to calculate exactly how much cash flow you need for freedom and how many properties it will take to get there.

Grab a calculator. This is where your dream becomes a plan.

Step 1: Calculate Your Monthly Expenses

First, you need to know how much money you need to live each month. Not what you make. What you spend.

List everything:

- Housing, including mortgage or rent, utilities, maintenance, and HOA.
- Transportation, including car payment, insurance, gas, and maintenance.
- Food, including groceries and dining out.
- Insurance, including health, life, and disability.
- Debt payments, including credit cards and student loans.
- Kids, including childcare, activities, and education.
- Lifestyle, including entertainment, travel, hobbies, hair care, and gym.
- Miscellaneous, including pets, subscriptions, holiday spending, and gifts.

Be honest. Do not lowball this. If you spend $8,000 per month, write $8,000.

Example: The Martinez Family

The Martinez family calculates their monthly expenses:

- Housing: $2,200
- Transportation: $800
- Food: $900
- Insurance: $400
- Debt: $300
- Kids: $500
- Lifestyle: $700
- Miscellaneous: $200

Total: $6,000 per month

That is their starting point. If they can generate $6,000 per month in passive cash flow from rental properties, they are free. But they are not done yet.

Step 2: Add a Buffer

Here is a mistake most people make: They calculate their exact expenses and assume that is enough. It is not.

You need a buffer for:

- Major repairs and capital expenses.
- Property vacancies.
- Medical emergencies.

- Inflation.
- Living a little.

Adding 30 to 40 percent to your monthly expenses is the right approach to ensure your freedom number is truly sustainable.

Martinez Family Adjusted Number:

$$\$6{,}000 \times 1.35 = \$8{,}100 \text{ per month}$$

That is their real cash flow freedom number: $8,100 per month.

Step 3: Calculate How Many Properties You Need

Now we need to figure out how many properties it takes to generate $8,100 per month in cash flow. This depends entirely on how much each property cash flows.

Here are three scenarios.

Scenario A: Conservative Properties at $250 per month cash flow each.

These are solid, bread-and-butter rentals in working-class neighborhoods. Not exciting, but reliable.

$$\$8{,}100 \div \$250 = 32 \text{ properties}$$

That sounds like a lot, and it is. But remember: you are building this over 10 to 15 years, and these properties are also appreciating and paying down mortgages.

Scenario B: Medium Properties at $400 per month cash flow each.

These might be small multifamily properties such as duplexes or triplexes, or well-located single-family homes in strong rental markets.

$$\$8,100 \div \$400 = 20 \text{ properties}$$

A significant portfolio, but far more achievable.

Scenario C: Strong Cash Flow Properties at $600 per month cash flow each.

These are fourplexes, small apartment buildings, or houses in high-demand rental markets with excellent numbers.

$$\$8,100 \div \$600 = 14 \text{ properties}$$

Now we are talking. Fourteen properties over 15 years is less than one per year.

The Real Math. It Is Better Than You Think.

Here is what most people miss: You do not need the full cash flow from day one to replace your income. You need it when you are ready to reach cash flow freedom.

Let's say you are 40 years old and want cash flow freedom at 55. That gives you 15 years.

If you buy just one property per year that cash flows $550 per month:

- Year 5: 5 properties × $550 = $2,750 per month, which is 34 percent toward freedom.

- Year 10: 10 properties × $550 = $5,500 per month, which is 68 percent toward freedom.

- Year 15: 15 properties × $550 = $8,250 per month, which equals 100 percent cash flow freedom.

But it gets better. By Year 15, your first properties have appreciated significantly, several mortgages are paid off or nearly paid off, and your cash flow per property has increased as rents rise while mortgages stay fixed.

That first property you bought in Year 1? It might be cash flowing $1,000 per month by Year 15.

Your actual cash flow at Year 15: $11,000 to $12,000 per month.

You exceeded your cash flow freedom number.

Timeline Examples at Different Ages

Age 30. The Long Game.

- Goal: Cash flow freedom at 50.

- Time horizon: 20 years.

- Strategy: Buy one property every 18 months, 13 to 14 properties total.

- Target: $500 per month cash flow per property.

- Year 10: 6 properties at $3,000 per month, which is 37 percent toward freedom.

- Year 15: 10 properties at $5,000 per month, which is 62 percent toward freedom.

- Year 20: 13 properties at $8,100 per month or more, reaching 100 percent cash flow freedom as several properties have paid-off or nearly paid-off mortgages.

At 30, you have time. You can be patient, buy right, and let compound growth do the heavy lifting.

Age 40. The Sprint.

- Goal: Cash flow freedom at 55.

- Time horizon: 15 years.

- Strategy: Buy one property per year.

- Target: $600 per month cash flow per property.

- Year 5: 5 properties at $3,000 per month, which is 37 percent toward freedom.

- Year 10: 10 properties at $6,000 per month, reaching 74 percent toward freedom as early mortgages pay down.

- Year 15: 15 properties at $9,000 per month or more, which is 111 percent of the freedom number, with multiple properties carrying significant equity.

At 40, you need to be more aggressive. One property per year is achievable if you stay focused.

Age 50. The Power Play.

- Goal: Cash flow freedom at 60.

- Time horizon: 10 years.

- Strategy: Buy one to two properties per year, or focus on higher cash flow properties.

- Target: $800 per month cash flow per property.

- Year 5: 7 to 8 properties at $5,600 to $6,400 per month, which is 69 to 79 percent toward freedom.

- Year 10: 12 to 15 properties at $9,600 to $12,000 per month, which is 118 to 148 percent cash flow freedom.

At 50, you likely have more capital, more income, and more urgency. You might also consider paying off mortgages faster to accelerate cash flow.

The Adjustment Factor. You Do Not Need 100 Percent Replacement.

Here is something most financial advisors will not tell you: You do not need to replace 100 percent of your current income to achieve cash flow freedom.

Why? Because once you are free, you no longer have commuting costs, work wardrobe expenses, or the habit of eating lunch out every day. Daycare costs may be gone if your children are older. Rental income is taxed differently than W2 income, which lowers your tax burden. You may also choose to downsize or relocate, reducing your housing costs.

Most people need only 60 to 75 percent of their current income to maintain their lifestyle in cash flow freedom.

So if the Martinez family currently makes $120,000 per year, or $10,000 per month, they may only need $6,500 to $8,100 per month to live comfortably without working.

Your Turn. Calculate Your Cash Flow Freedom Number.

Fill in the blanks:

My monthly expenses: $______________

Plus 35 percent buffer: $______________

My cash flow freedom number: $______________

Divided by average cash flow per property:
$______________

Number of properties I need: ______________

My current age: ______________

Target cash flow freedom age: ______________

Years to build: ______________

Properties needed ÷ Years to build = ______________
properties per year

Now you have a target. Is it achievable? Absolutely. Will it be easy? No. Is it worth it? That depends on how much you value cash flow freedom.

The Beauty of This Plan

Here is what makes this approach powerful.

1. **It is specific.** You are not guessing. You have a real cash flow target.

2. **It is flexible.** Life changes, cash flow changes, and you adjust.

3. **It is forgiving.** If you miss a year or two, you can catch up.

4. **It is realistic.** You are not trying to get rich overnight.

5. **It is proven.** Thousands of people have already achieved cash flow freedom this way, including me.

In the next chapter, we are going to talk about the mindset required to actually execute this plan. Knowing your cash flow freedom number is one thing. Having the discipline to buy and hold for decades is another.

Chapter 4: The Buy-and-Hold Mindset

Let me tell you about two investors.

Investor 1: Flipping Frank

Frank got into real estate in 2015. He watched HGTV, read a few books on flipping, and jumped in. Over the next eleven years, he flipped 55 houses. He had some wins, some losses, and a lot of stress.

In 2026, Frank sat down and calculated his net worth from all that activity: $240,000.

Not bad for eleven years of work, except Frank worked 60-hour weeks, dealt with contractors constantly, and aged 20 years in the process. He made money, but he did not build cash flow. He also missed out on beneficial IRS tax deductions, since he was never considered an investor by IRS standards. And he definitely did not achieve cash flow freedom.

Investor 2: Buy-and-Hold Betty

Betty got into real estate the same year as Frank, in 2015. But Betty's strategy was different. She bought one rental property per year. No flips, no wholesaling, no fancy strategies. Just buy, rent, and hold.

By 2026, Betty owned eleven properties:

- Total cash flow: $4,800 per month.
- Total equity from appreciation and mortgage paydown: $680,000.

- Time spent per month: 3 to 4 hours, since she uses property management.

Betty built more wealth than Frank, worked less, stressed less, and has $4,800 per month in cash flow whether she works or not. She is 59 percent of the way to cash flow freedom. Frank has to start over every time he wants to make money.

Why Flipping Will Not Get You to Cash Flow Freedom

Flipping can make you money. But it has fundamental problems.

1. **It is a job.** Every flip requires your time, energy, and attention. Stop flipping and you stop earning. No cash flow means no path to freedom.

2. **It is taxed as ordinary income.** Flip profits are taxed at your regular income rate, up to 37 percent, not capital gains rates of 15 to 20 percent.

3. **It is risky.** Markets shift, contractors disappear, and budgets blow up. One bad flip can wipe out three good ones.

4. **It does not scale.** You can only flip so many houses per year. There is a ceiling on your income.

5. **It does not build cash flow freedom.** At the end of 10 years of flipping, you may have cash in the bank. But if you stop flipping, the money stops coming. You are no closer to cash flow freedom than when you started.

Flipping is a hustle, not a path to freedom.

The Buy-and-Hold Advantage for Cash Flow Freedom

Buy-and-hold investing works in the opposite direction.

1. **It builds toward freedom.** Once the property is rented with a good tenant and managed properly, it generates cash flow on autopilot.

2. **Time accelerates your freedom.** The longer you hold, the more cash flow you build. Mortgages pay down, properties appreciate, and rents increase. Your path to freedom gets shorter every year.

3. **Tax advantages compound.** Depreciation, 1031 exchanges, and long-term capital gains treatment reward holders, not flippers. You keep more of your cash flow.

4. **Cash flow builds with every property.** Each property adds to your monthly cash flow freedom number. Ten properties means ten income streams bringing you closer to freedom.

5. **It creates true freedom.** After 20 years of buy-and-hold investing, you own properties free and clear, generating tens of thousands per month in cash flow. That is cash flow freedom.

The Formula. Time Plus Tenants Equals Cash Flow Freedom.

Here is the simple truth of rental real estate:
Time + tenants = cash flow freedom.

Your tenants pay your mortgage. Your tenants cover your expenses. Your tenants buy the property for you. Your tenants fund your freedom.

All you have to do is buy the right property, put a good tenant in it, and hold it for the long term. That is the whole strategy.

It is not exciting. It will not make you Instagram-famous. But it leads to cash flow freedom.

Overcoming the Get-Rich-Quick Mentality

We live in a culture that glorifies speed.

"I made $50K on this flip!"

"I wholesaled 10 deals this month!"

"I'm crushing it in real estate!"

And it is tempting to chase that. But here is what they do not show you:

- The 80-hour weeks.
- The deals that fell apart.
- The stress of carrying multiple projects.
- The fact that they will have to do it all over again next month.
- The fact that they are no closer to cash flow freedom than when they started.

Fast money feels good in the moment, but it does not build cash flow freedom.

The Marshmallow Test for Adults

There is a famous psychology experiment where children are offered one marshmallow now or two marshmallows if they wait 15 minutes. The children who could delay gratification went on to have better life outcomes, including better grades, better health, and better finances.

Buy-and-hold real estate is the marshmallow test for adults. You are choosing cash flow freedom in 15 years over a quick profit today. You are choosing passive income forever over active income for a few months.

Most people cannot do it. They get impatient. They chase the next shiny object. They sell too early.

But if you can be patient, if you can buy and hold, you will achieve cash flow freedom while 95 percent of people who work in real estate are still hustling.

The Three Temptations That Kill Your Path to Cash Flow Freedom

Even if you start with a buy-and-hold strategy, three temptations will try to derail you.

Temptation 1: Selling to take the profit

Your property appreciates $80,000 in five years. Someone offers to buy it and you think you should cash out. Here is why that destroys your path to freedom: you will pay capital gains taxes, you lose the monthly cash flow that property was generating, you lose the mortgage paydown that was happening, and you have to find another property to replace it. Unless you absolutely need the cash or the property has become a serious problem, hold it. Every property you sell delays your cash flow freedom.

Temptation 2: Refinancing to pull out equity and buy more

Your property has $100,000 in equity. You refinance, pull out $80,000, and use it to buy more properties. This works when the property still cash flows well after the refinance and you are using the capital to buy more cash-flowing properties. It fails when you over-leverage, destroy your cash flow, and create a house of cards that delays your freedom. Equity is valuable, but cash flow is freedom. Do not sacrifice cash flow to grow faster.

Temptation 3: Abandoning the strategy for something different

You have been buy-and-hold for three years. It is working, but it feels slow. You hear about someone making $100,000 flipping houses or $50,000 wholesaling and you think maybe you should try that. Do not. The graveyard of real estate investing is full of people who had a working strategy toward cash flow freedom and abandoned it to chase something shinier. Buy-and-hold is boring. It is supposed to be boring. Boring gets you to cash flow freedom.

The 10-Year Horizon

Here is the mindset shift that will change everything: Every property you buy, you are committing to hold for at least 10 years. Not "I'll see how it goes." Not "Maybe I'll sell if it appreciates." Not "I'll hold it unless something better comes along." Ten years, minimum.

Why? Because that is when cash flow freedom accelerates. In 10 years, your property has likely doubled in value, you have paid down 30 to 40 percent of the mortgage, your cash flow has increased as rents rise and mortgage payments stay fixed, and you have collected 120 months of rent moving you steadily toward freedom.

That is wealth. That is freedom. But only if you hold.

Your Commitment to Cash Flow Freedom

Before you buy your first property, make this commitment:

> *"I will buy rental properties with the intention of holding them for at least 10 years to build cash flow freedom. I will not sell because of market fluctuations, minor repairs, or impatience. I will focus on cash flow, not quick profits. I will let time and tenants build my path to freedom."*

If you can commit to this, you will achieve cash flow freedom while 90 percent of people who call themselves real estate investors are still stuck on the hamster wheel.

In the next section, we are moving from mindset to mechanics. We are going to talk about how to actually finance your first property, even if you think you do not have enough money.

PART 2:

BUILDING YOUR CASH FLOW

Chapter 5: Financing Your First Property

> *"I'd love to get into rental properties and build cash flow freedom, but I don't have enough money."*

I hear this constantly. And I understand it, because real estate requires capital. But here is the truth: You need less money than you think, and there are more ways to finance a property than you realize.

Let's break down exactly how to fund your first cash-flowing property.

How Much Money Do You Actually Need?

Start with a typical scenario: buying a $200,000 rental property.

Traditional Financing with 20 Percent Down

- Down payment: $40,000 (20 percent)
- Closing costs: $6,000 to $8,000 (3 to 4 percent)
- Reserves: $5,000 to $10,000 for repairs, vacancy, and cushion

Total cash needed: $51,000 to $58,000

That is not pocket change. But it is also not $200,000. You are getting a $200,000 cash-flowing asset for roughly $50,000. That is leverage working toward your freedom.

Owner-Occupied Financing with 3 to 5 Percent Down

If you are willing to live in the property first, you can use an FHA loan with 3.5 percent down or a conventional owner-occupied loan with 5 percent down.

Using the same $200,000 property:

- Down payment: $7,000 to $10,000
- Closing costs: $6,000 to $8,000
- Reserves: $5,000

Total cash needed: $18,000 to $23,000

Much more achievable. The requirement is that you live there for at least one year. This is how many investors start their path to cash flow freedom: buy a duplex, live in one side, rent the other. After a year, move out, rent both sides, and buy your next property. This strategy is called house hacking, and it is one of the smartest ways to start building cash flow.

Traditional Financing Options

Here are the standard ways to finance rental properties.

1. Conventional Loans

For investment properties:

- 15 to 20 percent down payment required.
- Interest rates typically 0.5 to 1 percent higher than owner-occupied loans.
- Maximum of 10 financed properties per person.

- Requires good credit, typically 680 or higher.
- Must show a debt-to-income ratio under 43 to 50 percent.

For owner-occupied loans that convert to rentals:

- 3 to 5 percent down payment.
- Lower interest rates.
- Must live in the property for 12 months.
- Can be repeated using a buy, live, rent, and repeat strategy to build cash flow.

2. Portfolio Loans Through Local Banks

Smaller banks and credit unions often hold loans in their own portfolio rather than selling them to Fannie Mae or Freddie Mac.

Advantages:

- More flexible lending criteria.
- Can finance more than 10 properties, which is important as you scale toward cash flow freedom.
- Faster closing.
- Relationship-based lending, meaning they get to know you and your track record.

Disadvantages:

- May require 25 to 30 percent down.
- Potentially higher interest rates.
- May have prepayment penalties.

Pro tip: Build relationships with two or three local banks. Once they see you are serious and responsible about building cash flow, they will compete for your business.

3. FHA Loans for House Hacking

FHA loans are government-backed loans for owner-occupants with the following requirements:

- 3.5 percent down payment.
- Must live in the property for 12 months.
- Property can be one to four units.
- Lower credit scores acceptable, typically 580 or higher.

The strategy is straightforward: buy a duplex, triplex, or fourplex, live in one unit, rent out the others, and let your tenants cover most or all of your mortgage. After 12 months, move out and buy another. This is the top way young investors with limited capital start building cash flow freedom.

4. VA Loans for Veterans

If you are a veteran, this is a significant advantage:

- Zero percent down payment.
- Lower interest rates.
- No mortgage insurance.
- Can buy up to a fourplex.

You can house hack with zero money down and start building cash flow immediately. If you are a veteran and not using this benefit, you are leaving money on the table.

5. DSCR Loans (Debt Service Coverage Ratio Loans)

DSCR loans are one of the most investor-friendly financing tools available today, and they are specifically designed for rental property purchases. Unlike conventional loans that qualify you based on your personal income, tax returns, and employment history, DSCR loans qualify you based entirely on the property's ability to generate income. The lender looks at one number: does the rental income cover the mortgage payment?

How the ratio works:

The DSCR is calculated by dividing the property's monthly rental income by its monthly debt obligation, which includes principal, interest, taxes, insurance, and any HOA fees. A DSCR of 1.0 means the rent exactly covers the payment. Most lenders require a minimum DSCR of 1.1 to 1.25, meaning the rent must exceed the total payment by at least 10 to 25 percent.

Example:

- Monthly rent: $2,000
- Total monthly payment (PITI): $1,600
- DSCR: $2,000 ÷ $1,600 = 1.25
- Result: Qualifies at most lenders.

Requirements:

- Typically 20 to 25 percent down payment.

- Credit score of 620 or higher, though better rates come with 680 or above.

- No personal income verification or tax returns required.

- Property must be non-owner-occupied and used as a rental.

- Available on single-family homes, condos, and two- to four-unit properties.

Why DSCR loans are valuable for building cash flow freedom:

- Self-employed investors and those with complex tax returns often show low taxable income, which makes conventional qualification difficult. DSCR loans eliminate that obstacle entirely.

- There is no limit tied to the number of properties you already own, making them ideal for scaling a portfolio.

- They close faster than conventional loans because there is no income documentation process.

- They are available from a wide range of non-bank lenders and mortgage brokers who specialize in investor financing.

The tradeoff is that DSCR loans typically carry interest rates slightly higher than conventional investment property loans, and they require a stronger down payment. But for investors who have been turned down by traditional lenders or who want a streamlined path to financing multiple properties, the DSCR loan is one of the most practical tools in the market today.

Creative Financing Strategies

If you do not have $50,000 saved, here are creative ways to get your first cash-flowing property.

1. Seller Financing

Sometimes sellers, especially older landlords who are ready to retire, will finance the property themselves. You negotiate terms directly with the seller, they act as the bank, and you make payments to them instead of a lender. Terms are negotiable, including interest rate, loan length, and balloon payment, and the arrangement often requires 10 to 20 percent down.

This works best when the seller owns the property free and clear, wants ongoing income rather than a lump sum, wants to defer capital gains taxes, or when the property is difficult to finance through traditional channels.

Example:

A $150,000 property with seller financing: 15 percent down ($22,500), 6 percent interest, 15-year amortization with a 5-year balloon payment. You make payments to the seller for five years, then refinance. The property cash flows from day one.

2. Lease Option

With a lease option, you lease the property with the right to buy it at a locked-in price. A portion of your rent goes toward the purchase price, giving you one to three years to secure financing and complete the purchase. You can rent the property to a tenant during that time and cash flow the difference.

Example:

A $180,000 property: you lease for $1,500 per month for two years, with $300 per month credited toward the purchase price. You rent the property for $1,800 per month, cash flowing $300 per month while building equity toward ownership.

3. Partnerships

You bring the expertise and hustle. Someone else brings the money. A common structure is a 50/50 split on cash flow and equity, with your partner providing the down payment and reserves while you find the deal, manage the property, and handle operations.

Keys to success: get everything in writing through an operating agreement, define roles clearly, agree on an exit strategy upfront, and work with people you trust.

Even at 50 percent ownership, you are building cash flow without using your own capital. Four partnership properties at $400 per month, with your 50 percent share equaling $200 each, produces $800 per month toward your freedom number.

4. Home Equity Line of Credit (HELOC)

If you own a home with equity, you can use a HELOC to fund your first rental.

Example:

Your home is worth $400,000 and you owe $250,000. At 80 percent loan-to-value, your HELOC limit is $70,000. You use $50,000 from the HELOC for the down payment and closing costs on a rental property.

The HELOC gives you quick access to capital, and you only pay interest on what you use. The risk is that it carries a variable interest rate and puts your primary home as collateral. The strategy is to use the HELOC for the down payment, then refinance the rental property after six to twelve months to pay back the HELOC, freeing it up for your next cash-flowing property.

5. 401(k) Loan

You can borrow from your 401(k) to fund a rental property. The rules allow you to borrow up to 50 percent of your vested balance with a maximum of $50,000, and the loan must typically be repaid within five years. The interest you pay goes back to your own account.

The main risks are the opportunity cost of money not invested in the market, the fact that the loan becomes due if you leave your job, and the possibility that defaulting triggers early withdrawal taxes and penalties. This option makes the most sense when you have a significant 401(k) balance and the property's cash flow can help you repay the loan quickly while building toward freedom.

6. Self-Directed IRA

A self-directed IRA allows you to use retirement funds to invest directly in real estate rather than being limited to stocks, bonds, and mutual funds. This is one of the most underutilized tools available to real estate investors.

How it works:

- You establish a self-directed IRA through a custodian that specializes in alternative investments.
- Your IRA purchases the rental property directly, and the property is owned by the IRA, not by you personally.

- All income from the property, including rent, flows back into the IRA tax-deferred or tax-free depending on whether it is a traditional or Roth self-directed IRA.

- All expenses, including repairs, taxes, and management fees, must be paid from the IRA as well.

Key rules to know:

- You cannot personally use or benefit from the property while it is held in the IRA.

- You cannot do business with disqualified persons, which includes yourself, your spouse, and certain family members.

- You cannot perform personal labor on the property, meaning no self-managed repairs.

- All transactions must be at arm's length.

Why this is powerful:

If you have a Roth self-directed IRA, your rental income and eventual sale proceeds grow completely tax-free. Over 10 to 20 years of cash flow and appreciation compounding inside a tax-free account, the numbers can be extraordinary.

This strategy requires working with a qualified self-directed IRA custodian and a CPA who understands the rules. The penalties for violating IRS guidelines are severe, so proper setup is essential. But for investors with substantial retirement savings who want to put those dollars to work in real estate, the self-directed IRA is one of the most powerful tools available.

7. Borrowing from Family

Family lending is one of the oldest and most practical financing strategies available, and it is often overlooked because people feel uncomfortable mixing family and money. But when structured properly, it can work extremely well for both parties.

How it works:

- A family member loans you the money for a down payment or the full purchase price.

- You agree on an interest rate, which should be at or above the IRS Applicable Federal Rate to avoid gift tax complications.

- You put the agreement in writing through a promissory note, just as you would with any lender.

- You make regular payments to your family member, giving them a reliable return on money that might otherwise be sitting in a low-yield savings account.

Why this can work for both sides:

- Your family member earns a better return than a savings account or CD.

- You get access to capital at potentially better terms than a bank.

- The property's cash flow can fund the repayment directly.

Keys to making it work:

- Put everything in writing. A handshake deal creates family conflict. A signed promissory note protects everyone.

- Be transparent about the risks. Your family member should understand that real estate investing carries risk, even when managed well.

- Pay on time, every time. Treating a family loan with the same discipline as a bank loan preserves both the relationship and your credibility.

- Work with an attorney to draft the promissory note and confirm the terms comply with IRS guidelines.

Family lending is not for everyone, and it is not appropriate if either party would be financially devastated by a loss. But for investors who have family members with idle capital and a willingness to support their goals, it can be the bridge that gets your first cash-flowing property off the ground.

Building Your War Chest

If you do not have the money yet, here is how to build it.

The 12-Month Savings Sprint

Let's say you need $25,000 for your first cash-flowing property. That is $2,083 per month for 12 months.

Here is how to get there:

Increase income:

- Take on a side gig, adding approximately $500 per month.

- Ask for a raise or promotion, adding approximately $300 per month.

- Sell items you no longer need and invest the proceeds immediately.

Decrease expenses:

- Cut subscriptions and memberships, saving approximately $100 per month.

- Reduce dining out, saving approximately $300 per month.

- Downgrade or eliminate a vehicle, saving approximately $400 per month.

- Move to less expensive housing temporarily, saving approximately $500 per month.

Total monthly savings: approximately $2,100

Is it easy? No. Is it worth it? Absolutely. One year of sacrifice can set up a lifetime of cash flow freedom.

Your Financing Action Plan

Here is what to do right now.

Step 1: Determine how much you can access

- Check your savings.

- Check your credit score, which is available free at annualcreditreport.com.

- Calculate available home equity if applicable.

- Check your 401(k) balance if you are considering that route.

Step 2: Choose your strategy.

- 20 percent down conventional loan if you have the capital.
- Owner-occupied financing if you are willing to house hack for cash flow.
- Creative financing if you are low on capital.
- Partnership if you have expertise but not money.

Step 3: Get pre-approved.

- Talk to two or three lenders.
- Get pre-approval letters.
- Understand your buying power.

Step 4: Build your reserves.

- Do not spend every dollar on the down payment.
- Keep $5,000 to $10,000 in reserves.
- Cash flow problems happen, so be prepared.

> *Note: Your reserves do not have to be cash sitting in a bank account. Access to a credit card with sufficient available credit can serve as your reserve buffer in a pinch. A card with $5,000 to $10,000 in available credit gives you a safety net for unexpected repairs or short-term vacancies while you build your cash reserves over time. This is not a long-term solution, but it is a legitimate and practical option for investors who are just getting started.*

You do not need to be rich to start building cash flow freedom. You just need to start.

In the next chapter, we are going to talk about where to buy, because location determines whether you build cash flow or buy yourself a problem.

Chapter 6: Finding the Right Market

You can do everything else right: find great financing, run perfect numbers, and manage well. But if you buy in the wrong market, you will struggle to build cash flow. Location is not just important. It is everything.

Let me show you what I mean.

Two Investors, Two Markets, Two Outcomes

Investor A bought a $150,000 house in a declining Rust Belt city. The property rents for $900 per month, which sounds decent.

Five years later:

- Property value: $140,000, a loss of $10,000.
- Vacancy rate: 40 percent due to constant tenant turnover.
- Repairs: $15,000 from an old house with constant issues.
- Neighborhood declining, making the property harder to rent each year.
- Monthly cash flow: negative, actively killing his path to freedom.

Investor B bought a $250,000 house in a growing Sunbelt suburb renting for $1,800 per month.

Five years later:

- Property value: $320,000, a gain of $70,000.

- Vacancy rate: 5 percent with quality tenants and low turnover.

- Repairs: $6,000 on a well-maintained, newer house.

- Neighborhood improving, making the property easier to rent with rising rents.

- Monthly cash flow: $450 per month, building steadily toward freedom.

Same strategy. Different markets. Completely different outcomes for cash flow freedom.

What Makes a Rental Market Strong for Cash Flow?

Not all markets are created equal. Here is what to look for.

1. Population Growth

More people means more demand for housing, which drives rising rents and property values and strengthens cash flow over time. You can find population data through Census reports, local economic reports, and the chamber of commerce.

Green flags:

- Population growing 1 to 2 percent or more annually.

- Young professionals moving into the area.

- New businesses opening.

- New construction, which signals market confidence.

Red flags:

- Population declining or stagnant.
- Businesses leaving.
- Aging population with no younger residents moving in.
- More homes for sale than there are buyers.

Austin, Nashville, Charlotte, and Raleigh all experienced massive population growth from 2010 to 2020 and saw rental markets explode with strong cash flow opportunities. By contrast, Detroit, Cleveland, and rural towns losing population saw property values stagnate or decline, making reliable cash flow much harder to build.

2. Job Growth and Diversity

Jobs attract people who can afford rent, which creates consistent cash flow. Look for markets with multiple major employers across diverse industries, a low unemployment rate under 5 percent, new companies moving in, and growing sectors such as healthcare, technology, and education.

Green flags:

- Major employers such as Amazon or Google opening offices.
- Medical centers or universities expanding.
- Military bases, which provide stable renters and steady cash flow.
- State capitals, where government employment provides stability.

Red flags:

- Single-industry towns, where one sector collapse can devastate the rental market.

- Factory closings.

- High unemployment.

- Brain drain, meaning young people are consistently leaving.

Huntsville, Alabama, which is anchored by the defense, aerospace, and technology industries, has thrived with strong rental cash flow. Coal country towns have not had that same stability.

3. Rent-to-Price Ratio

This is one of the most useful tools for identifying cash-flowing markets. Divide the monthly rent by the purchase price to get the ratio. A minimum of 0.7 percent is acceptable, 1.0 percent or higher is strong, and 1.5 percent or above, while rare, is excellent for cash flow freedom.

Examples:

- Market A: $200,000 house renting for $1,400 per month. $1,400 divided by $200,000 equals 0.7 percent. Barely works.

- Market B: $150,000 house renting for $1,500 per month. $1,500 divided by $150,000 equals 1.0 percent. Strong cash flow potential.

- Market C: $100,000 house renting for $1,200 per month. $1,200 divided by $100,000 equals 1.2 percent. Excellent cash flow and a faster path to freedom.

Higher ratios mean better cash flow potential and a faster journey to freedom. Strong ratios are typically found in Midwest cities such as Indianapolis, Columbus, and Kansas City, as well as smaller Sunbelt cities such as Augusta, Georgia and Mobile, Alabama.

Markets like San Francisco, New York, and Los Angeles have ratios in the 0.3 to 0.4 percent range, and Seattle, Boston, and Denver run 0.4 to 0.5 percent. You can build appreciation in those markets, but you will not build cash flow. This book is about cash flow freedom.

4. Landlord-Friendly Laws

State and local laws dramatically affect your success as a landlord and your ability to protect cash flow.

Landlord-friendly states include:

- Texas, with fast evictions and minimal regulations.
- Indiana, with strong tenant responsibility laws.
- Florida, which provides solid landlord protections.
- Tennessee, with a streamlined eviction process.
- Alabama, which is generally landlord-favorable.

Landlord-hostile states include:

- California, with rent control and notoriously difficult evictions.
- New York, with extensive tenant protections and long eviction timelines.
- New Jersey, which is expensive and strongly tenant-friendly.
- Oregon, which has strict rent control laws.

Research the eviction timeline, rent control laws, security deposit limits, required disclosures, and tenant protection laws in any market you consider. A great cash-flowing deal in a hostile landlord state can become a nightmare that derails your path to freedom.

You may find websites with tools for researching each state. Justia.com has a 50-State Survey on eviction laws you can easily search.

5. Crime and School Ratings

Crime:

- Check local crime statistics at CrimeReports.com and NeighborhoodScout.com.

- Visit the area at different times, including mornings, evenings, and weekends.

- Talk to local police about the neighborhood.

- Ask local property managers which areas to avoid.

Schools:

- Use GreatSchools.org and look for ratings of 7 or higher.

- Good schools attract families, who are typically stable tenants with lower turnover, which means more consistent cash flow.

- Poor schools make it harder to attract families, which often leads to more turnover and disrupted cash flow.

You do not need to buy in the best school district, but avoid the worst ones.

6. Days on Market and Vacancy Rates

Days on Market:

- Check Zillow and Realtor.com for average days on market.

- Under 30 days indicates a hot market.

- 30 to 60 days is a normal market.

- 60 days or more signals a weak market.

Rental Vacancy Rates:

- Check Census data or contact a local apartment association.

- Under 5 percent indicates strong demand and is excellent for cash flow.

- 5 to 6 percent is a healthy market.

- 7 percent or higher signals oversupply and weak demand, which threatens cash flow.

Low vacancy means you can rent quickly and raise rents over time, which accelerates your path to freedom.

Analyzing Neighborhoods Within a Market

Even in great markets, some neighborhoods work and others do not. Here is how to evaluate them.

The Drive-Through Test

Before you buy, drive the neighborhood and look for the following.

Green flags:

- Well-maintained homes.
- Children playing outside, which signals families and stability.
- Minimal trash or debris.
- Older residents maintaining their yards, which reflects pride of ownership.

Red flags:

- Boarded-up windows.
- Multiple houses for sale at the same time.
- Trash everywhere.
- Bars on windows.
- An abundance of For Rent signs, which indicates high turnover and cash flow problems.

Trust your instincts. If it does not feel safe, do not buy there.

The Walmart and Starbucks Test

It sounds simple, but it works. When national retailers such as Walmart, Target, or Starbucks open in an area, it signals growth and rising consumer demand. These companies conduct extensive market research before committing to a location. If they are investing, that is a meaningful signal.

Also look for new grocery stores, chain restaurants, and new gas stations. These all indicate population growth and market confidence, which is good for cash flow.

The Rental Comp Test

Search Zillow, Apartments.com, or Zumper for rentals in the target neighborhood and look at how many are available, how long they have been listed, what they are charging for rent, and what condition they are in. If you find 20 rentals that have been sitting for 60 days or more, that is a serious red flag for cash flow.

Local vs. Out-of-State Investing

Should you invest where you live or buy out of state? The honest answer is that it depends.

Local investing

The advantages are that you can drive by properties easily, you know the area, you can meet contractors and tenants in person, and you face lower risk because you are on familiar ground. The disadvantages are that your local market may not cash flow well, inventory may be limited, and emotional attachment can cause you to overthink decisions. Local investing is best for beginners, investors in cash-flowing markets, and those who prefer a hands-on approach.

Out-of-state investing

The advantages are access to stronger cash-flowing markets, more inventory options, and the discipline that comes from being forced to build systems. The disadvantages are higher risk from unfamiliarity, the required cost of property management at 8 to 10 percent of rent, difficulty verifying property condition, and the occasional need to travel for major issues. Out-of-state investing is best for experienced investors, those in expensive markets, and those building larger portfolios toward cash flow freedom.

My recommendation:

Start local if possible. Learn the process close to home where mistakes are cheaper and you can build your first streams of cash flow with less complexity. Once you have completed one to three local deals and understand the business, then expand out of state for better numbers.

The exception is if you live in San Francisco, New York, or another market where cash flow is simply not achievable. In that case, invest out of state from day one, but partner with an experienced local investor or hire an excellent property manager before you start.

The Top Rental Markets for Cash Flow

Based on population growth, job growth, landlord laws, and rent-to-price ratios, here are strong markets for building cash flow as of 2026.

Tier 1: Strong All-Around for Cash Flow

- Indianapolis, Indiana
- Kansas City, Missouri
- Columbus, Ohio
- Memphis, Tennessee
- Jacksonville, Florida
- San Antonio, Texas
- Oklahoma City, Oklahoma
- Charlotte, North Carolina

Tier 2: Good Growth with Lower Cash Flow, but Still Builds Toward Freedom

- Nashville, Tennessee, which is appreciating quickly but becoming expensive.
- Austin, Texas, which offers great growth but has elevated prices.
- Raleigh-Durham, North Carolina
- Tampa, Florida
- Phoenix, Arizona

Tier 3: High Cash Flow with Less Appreciation, Providing a Faster Path to Freedom

- Birmingham, Alabama
- Little Rock, Arkansas
- Wichita, Kansas
- Fort Wayne, Indiana
- Mobile, Alabama

Markets to Approach with Caution

- Any California city, due to tenant laws, rent control, and high taxes.
- New York, due to extensive regulations and tenant protections.
- Chicago, due to high taxes, regulations, and population decline in parts of the city.
- Declining Rust Belt cities, where population loss threatens long-term cash flow.

Markets change over time. These are trends, not guarantees. Always do your own research before committing.

Your Market Selection Checklist

Before you buy in a market, work through this checklist.

☐ Population growing 1 percent or more annually.

☐ Job growth with diverse employers.

☐ Rent-to-price ratio of 0.8 percent or higher. A higher ratio means a faster path to cash flow freedom.

☐ Landlord-friendly laws.

☐ Acceptable crime statistics.

☐ School ratings of 6 or higher in target neighborhoods.

☐ Vacancy rates under 7 percent.

☐ Properties renting within 30 to 45 days.

☐ Neighborhood passes the drive-through test.

☐ Multiple property managers available, especially important for out-of-state investing.

If you check eight or more boxes, it is a strong market for building cash flow. If you check fewer than six, keep looking.

Do Not Overthink It

Here is the truth: You can build cash flow freedom in dozens of markets across the United States. You do not need the perfect market. You need a good market where the numbers work and properties cash flow.

Analysis paralysis kills more investors' paths to freedom than bad markets ever will.

Pick a market that checks most of the boxes, buy your first cash-flowing property, learn from the experience, and move forward.

In the next chapter, we are getting into the numbers: how to analyze a deal and know whether it is going to build your cash flow or cost you money.

Chapter 7: The Numbers That Matter

This is where most investors fail. They get emotional about a property, fall in love with the kitchen, the neighborhood, or the potential, and forget to run the actual numbers.

Let me be direct: If the numbers do not work, you are not building cash flow. Walk away. It does not matter how attractive the property is. It does not matter if your agent says it's a great opportunity. It does not matter if you have already gotten emotionally invested.

The numbers do not lie. Building cash flow freedom is a numbers game.

The Only Three Questions That Matter

When analyzing a rental property, you need to answer three questions.

1. **Does it cash flow?** Will it put money in your pocket each month toward freedom?

2. **Can I afford it?** Do I have the down payment, reserves, and ability to cover expenses?

3. **Is it a good investment?** Will it build wealth over time?

Question 1: Does It Cash Flow?

Cash flow is the money left over after all expenses are paid. The formula is straightforward:

Gross Rent - All Expenses - Mortgage = Cash Flow

Let's work through a real example.

Sample Property Analysis

Purchase Price: $180,000

Down Payment (20 percent): $36,000

Loan Amount: $144,000

Interest Rate: 7 percent

Term: 30 years

Monthly Rent: $1,650

Step 1: Calculate Monthly Expenses.

Mortgage Payment (Principal and Interest): $958

Use a mortgage calculator online to get this number. I use the one on Bankrate.com's website.

Property Taxes: $200 per month

Check county tax records for the exact amount and divide the annual figure by 12.

Insurance: $100 per month

Call insurance agents for quotes before you buy.

Property Management (10 percent): $165 per month

Budget for this even if you self-manage. Your time has value.

Vacancy Reserve (7 to 10 percent): $125 per month

Properties sit empty sometimes. Budget for it.

Maintenance Reserve (10 percent): $165 per month

Things break. Always.

CapEx Reserve (5 to 7 percent): $100 per month

Capital expenditures cover roof, HVAC, and water heater replacements.

Total Monthly Expenses: **$1,813**

Step 2: Calculate Cash Flow.

Gross Rent: $1,650

Total Expenses: $1,813

Monthly Cash Flow: -$163

This deal does not work. You would be losing $163 per month. This property moves you away from cash flow freedom. It is a hard pass.

What If We Adjust the Numbers?

Suppose you negotiate the price down or find a property that rents for more.

Purchase Price: $160,000 (negotiated down)

Down Payment: $32,000

Loan Amount: $128,000

Monthly Rent: $1,700 (stronger rental market)

New Mortgage Payment: $851

Other Expenses: $855 (management, taxes, insurance, reserves)

Total Expenses: $1,706

Cash Flow: $1,700 minus $1,706 = negative $6 per month

Still not ideal, but close. If rent increases by $50 or expenses drop slightly, this property becomes cash flow positive and begins building toward freedom.

A Market with Stronger Cash Flow Potential

Purchase Price: $120,000 (Midwest or secondary market)

Monthly Rent: $1,400

Down Payment: $24,000

Loan Amount: $96,000

Mortgage: $639

Taxes: $150

Insurance: $80

Property Management: $140

Vacancy Reserve: $105

Maintenance Reserve: $140

CapEx Reserve: $85

Total Expenses: **$1,339**

Cash Flow: **$1,400 minus $1,339 = $61 per month**

This works. Not spectacular, but it is positive cash flow building toward your freedom.

The 1% Rule. A Quick Screening Tool.

Before you run detailed numbers, use the 1% rule to screen deals quickly. Divide the monthly rent by the purchase price. If the result is 1 percent or higher, the deal is worth analyzing further and is likely to cash flow. If it falls below

0.8 percent, it probably will not cash flow well enough to justify the effort.

Examples:

- A $150,000 property renting for $1,500 per month equals 1.0 percent. Worth analyzing.

- A $200,000 property renting for $1,600 per month equals 0.8 percent. Borderline. Analyze carefully.

- A $250,000 property renting for $1,800 per month equals 0.72 percent. Likely will not cash flow and will not build freedom.

The 1% rule is not perfect, but it saves you time by eliminating weak deals before you invest hours in a full analysis.

Question 2: Can I Afford It?

Cash flow is only half the equation. You also need to confirm that you can afford to buy and hold the property.

What you need upfront:

- Down payment, which is 20 percent for an investment property or less if owner-occupied.

- Closing costs, typically 3 to 5 percent of the purchase price.

- Reserves of $5,000 to $10,000 minimum.

- First-month repairs and capital improvements, budgeting $3,000 to $5,000 for immediate fixes.

Example using a $150,000 property:

> Down Payment: $30,000
>
> Closing Costs: $5,000
>
> Reserves: $7,000
>
> Immediate Repairs: $3,000
>
> **Total Needed:** **$45,000**

Ask yourself honestly whether you can afford $45,000 while still maintaining an emergency fund. If not, wait or look for a less expensive property.

What if cash flow is slightly negative?

Some experienced investors accept a small negative cash flow of $50 to $100 per month when the property is in a rapidly appreciating market, rents are rising quickly, they have W2 income to cover the shortfall, or they plan to pay down the mortgage faster than the standard schedule.

For beginners building toward cash flow freedom, do not do this. Only buy cash-flowing properties. Once you have three to five properties and understand the business, you can begin taking calculated risks.

Question 3: Is It a Good Investment?

Cash flow tells you if the property pays you monthly. These additional metrics tell you whether it is a sound long-term investment.

1. Cash-on-Cash Return

This measures your annual cash flow relative to the actual cash you invested.

Annual Cash Flow divided by Total Cash Invested, multiplied by 100 = Cash-on-Cash Return

Example:

Annual Cash Flow: $732 ($61 per month times 12)

Total Cash Invested: $45,000

Cash-on-Cash Return: 1.6 percent

That is not a strong standalone number. But cash-on-cash return is only one part of the picture.

Target ranges:

- 5 to 7 percent is acceptable, beating savings accounts and building toward freedom.

- 8 to 10 percent is good, beating inflation and building real wealth.

- 12 percent or higher is excellent and rare in today's market.

Remember the other wealth-building pillars working alongside cash flow. On the same $150,000 property, you are also receiving approximately $1,100 per year in mortgage paydown from tenant payments and approximately $4,500 per year in appreciation at 3 percent. Combined with $732 in cash flow, that is $6,332 in total wealth increase in Year 1.

Dividing $6,332 by the $45,000 invested produces a 14 percent total return. That is building real wealth and moving steadily toward cash flow freedom.

2. Cap Rate (Capitalization Rate)

Cap rate measures the property's return assuming you paid all cash with no mortgage.

Net Operating Income divided by Purchase Price, multiplied by 100 = Cap Rate

Net Operating Income, or NOI, is gross rent minus operating expenses, not including the mortgage payment.

Example:

Gross Rent: $16,800 per year

Operating Expenses: $7,020 per year

NOI: $9,780

Cap Rate: $9,780 divided by $120,000 = 8.15 percent

What is a good cap rate?

- 4 to 6 percent is low, typical of expensive markets with lower cash flow or high-demand properties.

- 7 to 9 percent is good and produces solid returns for cash flow freedom.

- 10 percent or higher is found in cheaper markets and carries either higher risk or higher returns.

Cap rates vary by market. Do not compare a New York property at 4 percent to an Indianapolis property at 10 percent. They are entirely different games.

3. Debt Service Coverage Ratio

The Debt Service Coverage Ratio tells you whether the property's income covers the mortgage payment.

Net Operating Income divided by Annual Mortgage Payment = DSCR

Example:

NOI: $9,780

Annual Mortgage: $7,668 ($639 times 12)

DSCR: $9,780 divided by $7,668 = 1.28

What you want:

- A DSCR above 1.25 means the property easily covers the mortgage and is safe for building cash flow.

- A DSCR between 1.0 and 1.25 means the property covers the mortgage, but the margin is tight.

- A DSCR below 1.0 means the property does not cover the mortgage. This destroys cash flow and puts your portfolio at risk.

Most lenders require a minimum DSCR of 1.20 to 1.25.

The Deal Analysis Worksheet

Use this template for every property you analyze. Run the numbers before you fall in love with the property.

PROPERTY ADDRESS: _______________________

PURCHASE ANALYSIS

Purchase Price: $______________

Down Payment (_______ percent): $______________

Loan Amount: $______________

Interest Rate: ______________ percent

Loan Term: ______________ years

INCOME

Monthly Rent: $______________

Other Income (laundry, parking, etc.):
$______________

Gross Monthly Income: $______________

EXPENSES

Mortgage (Principal and Interest): $______________

Property Taxes: $______________

Insurance: $______________

HOA (if applicable): $______________

Property Management (10 percent): $______________

Vacancy Reserve (7 to 10 percent): $______________

Maintenance Reserve (10 percent): $______________

CapEx Reserve (5 to 7 percent): $______________

Total Monthly Expenses: $______________

CASH FLOW

Gross Income: $______________

Total Expenses: $______________

Monthly Cash Flow: $______________

Annual Cash Flow: $______________

RETURN METRICS

Cash-on-Cash Return: ______________ percent

Cap Rate: ______________ percent

DSCR: ______________

1% Rule Check: ______________ percent

CASH FLOW FREEDOM IMPACT

My current monthly cash flow: $____________

This property adds: $____________

New total monthly cash flow: $____________

My cash flow freedom number: $____________

Percentage toward freedom: ____________ percent

DECISION:

☐ Buy. This property builds cash flow.

☐ Pass. This property does not cash flow.

☐ Renegotiate.

When to Walk Away

Walk away if any of the following are true:

- Cash flow is negative, unless you have a very specific strategy and significant experience to back it up.

- The DSCR is under 1.2.

- The cash-on-cash return is under 5 percent and there is no meaningful appreciation potential.

- The total cash needed exceeds your budget.

- The deal fails the 1% rule by a significant margin.

- Repairs needed exceed 15 percent of the purchase price.

- You have a bad feeling about the neighborhood, a.k.a. you wouldn't live there.

There will always be another deal. Do not force it. Only buy properties that move you toward cash flow freedom.

Cash Flow Per Property. The Metric That Drives Freedom.

As discussed in Chapter 2, cash flow per property matters more than number of properties. Consider these two portfolios.

- Twenty properties averaging $100 per month each equals $2,000 per month toward freedom.
- Eight properties averaging $400 per month each equals $3,200 per month toward freedom.

The second portfolio delivers more monthly cash flow, fewer headaches, less management, and a faster path to freedom. Consider the cost difference between replacing 20 roofs versus 8. Always optimize for cash flow per property, not property count.

Your First Deal Will Be Scary

Every investor goes through the same experience with their first property: fear that they are making a mistake, doubt that the numbers are right, anxiety about whether the property will rent, and second-guessing at every step.

This is normal. Do your analysis. If the numbers work and the property cash flows, move forward.

You will never have perfect information. You will never have zero risk. But if you wait for the perfect deal, you will never start building cash flow freedom.

In the next chapter, we are walking through the actual purchase process, including making offers, scheduling inspections, and closing on your first cash-flowing rental property.

Chapter 8: Your First Purchase

You have found a property. The numbers work. It cash flows. Now what?

This chapter walks you through the actual process of buying your first cash-flowing rental property, from making the offer to holding the keys and starting your journey toward cash flow freedom.

Step 1: Making an Offer That Wins Without Overpaying

In real estate, everything is negotiable. The list price is just a starting point.

How to Determine Your Offer Price

Start with your numbers. That deal analysis worksheet from Chapter 7 tells you the maximum purchase price for the property to hit your cash flow target.

Example:

You want a minimum of $200 per month in cash flow to build toward freedom. You run the numbers and determine:

- At $150,000, the property cash flows $250 per month.
- At $160,000, the property cash flows $150 per month.
- Your maximum price is $155,000.

List price: $165,000

Your offer: Start at $145,000 to $150,000

Why offer below asking price? First, it leaves room to negotiate up. Second, you might get it accepted, because motivated sellers do exist. Third, it establishes that you are serious but disciplined about building cash flow.

What if it is a hot market and properties are selling over asking?

Then you have three choices.

1. **Offer at or slightly above asking price** if the numbers still work and the property cash flows.

2. **Walk away** and find a different market with better cash flow potential.

3. **Wait out the market.** If the market is overheated, patience is a strategy. Markets cool down. Prices soften. Sellers become more motivated. There is no rule that says you have to buy today. Waiting six to twelve months in a frothy market can mean the difference between a cash-flowing property and an expensive mistake.

Never overpay just because you are afraid to lose a deal. Overpaying destroys cash flow and delays your path to freedom.

Writing a Strong Offer

Your offer should include the following elements.

1. Purchase Price

Start 5 to 10 percent below asking if the market allows. Adjust based on days on market, since 100 or more days means more negotiating room; condition, since needed repairs justify a lower offer; and comparable sales, which you can pull from Zillow or Realtor.com.

2. Earnest Money Deposit

Typically $1,000 to $5,000. This shows you are serious and is returned to you if the deal falls through, provided you have proper contingencies in place.

3. Financing Contingency

This offer is contingent on the buyer obtaining financing. This protects you. If you cannot secure a loan, you get your earnest money back.

4. Inspection Contingency

This offer is contingent on a satisfactory home inspection within 10 days. This is critical. Never waive an inspection unless you have significant construction experience and know exactly what you are looking at. Hidden problems destroy cash flow.

5. Appraisal Contingency

This offer is contingent on the property appraising at or above the purchase price. This protects you if the property does not appraise. You can renegotiate or walk away.

6. Closing Date

Typically 30 to 45 days for financed purchases, and faster if paying cash.

7. Seller Concessions (Optional)

You can ask the seller to pay a portion of your closing costs. For example: Seller to contribute $3,000 toward buyer's closing costs. This is useful if you are short on cash but can absorb a slightly higher purchase price.

The Negotiation Process

Here is how a typical negotiation plays out:

> You offer: $145,000
>
> Seller counters: $162,000
>
> You counter: $150,000
>
> Seller counters: $157,000
>
> You counter: $153,000 as your final offer
>
> Seller accepts $155,000, or you walk away

Key negotiation principles to keep in mind:

1. **Know your walk-away number.** If it does not cash flow, it does not move you toward freedom. Walk away.

2. **Do not get emotional.** This is a business transaction that is building your cash flow.

3. **Be willing to walk.** The seller can sense desperation.

4. **Use time to your advantage.** If the property has been sitting for 90 or more days, the seller is motivated.

5. **Find out the seller's motivation.** Are they relocating? Did they inherit the property? Are they a tired landlord? Understanding their situation gives you leverage.

Multiple Offer Situations

If you are in a competitive market with multiple offers, you have three options.

Option 1: Offer asking price with strong terms

- Larger earnest money deposit.
- Shorter inspection period.
- Flexible closing date that matches the seller's needs.
- Pre-approval letter included with the offer.

Option 2: Escalation clause

State in your offer that you will escalate $1,000 above any competing offer up to a stated maximum. Only use this if your maximum number still produces acceptable cash flow.

Option 3: Write a personal letter

Some sellers, especially older landlords, care about who is buying their property. A short letter explaining that you are a long-term buy-and-hold investor building cash flow freedom rather than a flipper can sometimes make the difference.

Step 2: The Home Inspection. Your Cash Flow Protection.

Once your offer is accepted, you typically have 7 to 14 days to inspect the property. Do not skip this step. Hidden problems destroy cash flow, and this inspection protects your path to freedom.

Hiring an Inspector

Expect to pay $300 to $500 for an inspection that takes 2 to 4 hours. The inspector will examine the foundation and structure, roof condition and age, electrical system, plumbing, HVAC system, windows and doors, drainage and grading, and pests including termites.

To find a qualified inspector, ask your real estate agent for recommendations, check Google reviews, verify they are licensed and certified, and confirm they carry errors and omissions insurance.

Attend the inspection in person

Walk through with the inspector. Ask questions. Here is what to watch for.

Major issues that can be deal-breakers:

- Foundation cracks or settling.
- Roof needing replacement, which typically costs $8,000 to $15,000.
- Electrical panel issues or outdated knob-and-tube wiring.
- Plumbing problems such as galvanized pipes or sewer line issues.
- HVAC system that is dead or failing, typically costing $5,000 to $10,000 to replace.
- Mold, asbestos, or lead paint.
- Structural damage.

Minor issues that are negotiable:

- Leaky faucets.

- Cracked outlets.
- Missing weather stripping.
- Loose handrails.
- Cosmetic issues.

After the Inspection

You have four options after receiving the inspection report.

Option 1: Request repairs

Ask the seller to repair specific items, such as fixing a roof leak or replacing the water heater, before closing. This works best when the seller is motivated and the issues are moderate in scope.

Option 2: Request a credit

Ask the seller for a closing credit to cover the cost of repairs. This is often the better option because you control the work, choose the contractor, and know the job is done correctly. Be aware that you will need available cash to complete the repairs after closing.

Option 3: Renegotiate the price

If the inspection revealed $15,000 in needed repairs that were not apparent upfront, use that information to reduce your offer accordingly.

Option 4: Walk away

If the inspection reveals major problems and the seller will not negotiate, walk away. Your earnest money is protected by the inspection contingency. Do not let a problem property destroy your path to cash flow freedom.

The $5,000 Rule:

If needed repairs are under $5,000, factor them into your cash reserves and handle them after closing without renegotiating. If repairs exceed $5,000, renegotiate or walk.

Step 3: The Appraisal

Your lender will order an appraisal to confirm the property is worth what you agreed to pay. Expect to pay $400 to $600, and plan for a one to two week turnaround after offer acceptance.

Three Possible Outcomes

Outcome 1: Appraises at or above purchase price

The deal moves forward without complications.

Outcome 2: Appraises below purchase price

This is a problem. Your lender will only loan based on the appraised value, not the contract price.

Example:

Agreed purchase price:	$160,000
Appraised value:	$150,000
20% down based on appraisal:	$30,000
Loan amount:	$120,000
Amount owed to seller:	$160,000

You must bring $40,000 to closing instead of $32,000.

Your options are to bring the additional $8,000 in cash, renegotiate the price down to $150,000, or walk away using the appraisal contingency.

If you offered asking price in a hot market, low appraisals are common. Always keep extra cash available or be prepared to renegotiate.

Outcome 3: Appraises above purchase price

If the appraisal comes in at $170,000 and you are paying $160,000, you have instant equity. This is rare, but it means more options for building cash flow down the road.

Step 4: Final Walkthrough

One to two days before closing, do a final walkthrough of the property. Confirm that all agreed repairs were completed, the property is in the same condition as when you made your offer, any appliances included in the sale are still present, utilities are on so you can test them, and there is no new damage.

If something is wrong, address it before closing. Once you sign, it becomes your problem and could directly impact your cash flow.

Step 5: Closing Day

This is the day you officially become a property owner and start building cash flow freedom.

What to bring:

- Government-issued ID.

- Cashier's check or wire transfer for the down payment and closing costs.
- Proof of homeowner's insurance.

What you will sign:

Expect to sign 50 to 100 pages of documents, including the Closing Disclosure showing all costs and fees, the Promissory Note as your promise to repay the loan, the Deed of Trust or Mortgage giving the lender a lien on the property, title documents, disbursement authorizations, and various required disclosures. Read everything. If the numbers do not match what you were quoted, stop and ask questions before signing.

Closing Costs Breakdown

Lender fees:

- Origination fee: 0.5 to 1 percent of the loan amount.
- Underwriting fee: $400 to $800.
- Appraisal: $400 to $800.
- Credit report: $25 to $50.

Title and escrow fees:

- Title search: $200 to $400.
- Title insurance: $500 to $2,000.
- Escrow or settlement fee: $500 to $1,000.
- Recording fees: $100 to $300.

Prepaid and escrow items:

- Property taxes, prorated to the closing date.

- Homeowner's insurance, first year premium.
- HOA dues if applicable.

Total closing costs typically run 3 to 5 percent of the purchase price. On a $150,000 property, expect to pay $4,500 to $7,500.

Step 6: After Closing. The First 48 Hours.

Congratulations. You own your first cash-flowing rental property, and your journey to cash flow freedom has begun. Here is what to do immediately.

Day 1:

☐ Change the locks immediately. You do not know who has copies of the existing keys.

☐ Turn on utilities in your name if not already done.

☐ Confirm your landlord insurance policy is active.

☐ Take photos of the entire property, inside and out, for your records.

☐ Set up an LLC or business entity if you have not already done so. (more on this later)

☐ Open a separate bank account for this property to track cash flow independently.

☐ Create a file, digital or physical, for all property documents.

Week 1:

☐ Have your own contractor assess the property and identify repairs beyond what the inspection covered.

☐ Build a punch list of needed repairs and updates.

☐ Get quotes from at least two contractors for larger items.

☐ Order any appliances or materials needed.

☐ Begin marketing the property for rent if it is not already occupied.

☐ Set up a rent collection system using a platform such as Venmo, Zelle, or a dedicated property management software.

Weeks 2 to 4:

☐ Complete repairs and updates.

☐ Deep clean the property.

☐ Schedule professional photos for the rental listing.

☐ List the property for rent.

☐ Screen potential tenants carefully to protect your cash flow.

☐ Execute the lease agreement.

☐ Collect the first month's rent and security deposit.

☐ Complete a move-in inspection with the tenant and document the condition in writing.

Your First Repair Budget

Even if the property appears to need nothing, budget $3,000 to $5,000 for immediate improvements. Typical first-month expenses include:

- Paint: $500 to $1,500
- Deep cleaning: $200 to $400
- Landscaping cleanup: $200 to $500
- Minor plumbing fixes: $200 to $500
- Minor electrical work: $200 to $400
- Lock changes: $100 to $200
- Appliance upgrades if needed: $500 to $2,000

Do not over-improve. Your tenants do not need granite countertops or premium finishes. Make the property clean, safe, and functional. Over-improving kills your cash flow returns.

The Emotional Rollercoaster of Your First Purchase

Here is what you will feel along the way.

During the offer: Excitement and fear.

During the inspection: Panic about everything that shows up in the report.

Before closing: "What am I doing? Should I back out?"

After closing: Relief, followed immediately by "Oh no, what have I done?"

First month: Buyer's remorse and anxiety about finding tenants.

First rent check: "This is amazing. I'm building cash flow freedom. Why didn't I do this sooner?"

Five years later: "I should have bought two. I'd be closer to freedom."

This is normal. Every investor goes through it. Push through.

What If Something Goes Wrong?

What if the deal falls through?

It happens. Financing falls through, the appraisal comes in low, or the inspection reveals major issues. With proper contingencies in place, you get your earnest money back and move on to the next property. Your path to cash flow freedom takes a little longer, but it does not end.

What if I overpay?

If you are holding long term, meaning 10 or more years, a slight overpayment gets erased by appreciation and mortgage paydown. Do not stress over it. Learn from it and adjust on the next purchase. As long as the property cash flows, you are still building toward freedom.

What if I cannot find a tenant?

If the property is in a decent area, priced correctly, and clean, you will find a tenant within 30 to 60 days. One or two months of vacancy will not destroy your path to cash flow freedom. Be patient and be responsive.

What if I realize I made a mistake?

You probably did not. But if you did, you have options: hold and learn from the experience, sell and break even or take a small loss, or rent it out and let time work in your favor. Very few real estate mistakes are unfixable with time. And as long as the property cash flows, it is still building your freedom.

The One Thing That Matters Most

Your first property does not have to be perfect. It just has to cash flow.

You will make mistakes. You will overpay a little. You will miss things in the inspection. You will stress about tenants. That is all normal and expected.

What matters is that you bought it. You took action. You are now building cash flow.

The second property will be easier. The third will be easier still. By the fifth, you will wonder why you were ever nervous.

But none of that happens unless you buy the first one and start generating that first stream of cash flow toward freedom.

In the next section, we are moving from buying your first property to building your portfolio, covering how to scale from one property to ten, fifteen, or twenty and accelerate your path to cash flow freedom.

PART 3:
SCALING YOUR CASH FLOW

Chapter 9: Managing for Maximum Cash Flow

You bought the property. Now you need to manage it without it stealing back your freedom.

This chapter is about systems: how to run your rentals efficiently, keep cash flow high, and avoid the nightmare tenant situations you hear about. Good management protects your cash flow. Bad management destroys it.

The Big Decision. Self-Management vs. Property Management.

First question: Are you going to manage the property yourself or hire a property manager? Here is how both options break down.

Option 1: Self-Management
Advantages:

- Save 8 to 10 percent of rent monthly, which means more cash flow toward freedom.
- Your funds are available as soon as the tenant pays, without much delay.
- Direct control over tenant selection and repairs.
- You have an eye on repairs and know what will be needed sooner.
- You learn the business intimately.
- Better cash flow, especially early on when every dollar counts toward freedom.

Disadvantages:

- You are on call around the clock, at least in theory.
- You handle tenant issues, late rent, and maintenance calls personally.
- Time commitment of 3 to 10 hours per property per month.
- Emotional involvement, because tenants will frustrate you.

Best for:

- Your first one to three properties.
- Properties within 30 minutes of your home.
- Investors with time and a willingness to learn.
- Investors who need maximum cash flow to reach freedom faster.

Option 2: Property Management

Cost is typically 8 to 10 percent of monthly rent, sometimes with a minimum per property.

What they do:

- Market and list the property.
- Screen tenants, which protects your cash flow.
- Collect rent.
- Handle maintenance calls.
- Coordinate repairs.

- Enforce lease terms.
- Handle evictions if needed.
- Provide monthly statements and tax documents.

Advantages:

- You are mostly hands-off.
- They handle tenant issues.
- Professional systems are already in place.
- Scales easily; they manage 10 properties as readily as one.
- Protects your time, which is the entire point of cash flow freedom.

Disadvantages:

- Costs 8 to 10 percent of rent monthly, which reduces cash flow.
- Quality varies dramatically from one company to the next.
- Less control over tenant selection and repairs.
- Some property managers are poor operators and will need to be monitored.

Best for:

- Out-of-state properties.
- Investors with five or more properties.
- Investors with demanding full-time jobs.
- Investors who value time over maximum cash flow.

- Investors approaching or already in cash flow freedom.

My Recommendation

For your first one to three properties, self-manage if possible. You will learn the business, build your systems, and maximize cash flow to reach freedom faster. Starting with property four, transition to professional management. Your time is better spent finding the next cash-flowing deal than handling maintenance calls. You are building cash flow freedom, not a management job.

The exception: If you live in a high-cost area and invest out of state, use property management from day one.

The other exception: If you work in real estate, say as a real estate sales professional, it might make sense to self-manage since you are in the industry.

Tenant Screening. Protecting Your Cash Flow.

Here is a truth that will save you thousands of dollars and accelerate your path to freedom: A good tenant is worth ten times more than a good deal.

You can buy the perfect property at the perfect price, but if you put a bad tenant in it, you will lose money, lose sleep, and destroy your cash flow. Bad tenants equal destroyed cash flow and a delayed path to freedom.

Here is how to screen tenants properly.

Your Tenant Screening Criteria

Set your standards before you start showing the property. These are the non-negotiables for protecting cash flow.

1. Credit Score

A credit score tells you whether someone pays their bills. It is not a perfect measure, but it is predictive of rent payment reliability. Keep in mind that a lower score does not automatically disqualify an applicant. Many good tenants have damaged credit due to a recent divorce, a previous illness that caused them to miss work, or a job loss that has since been resolved and replaced. Evaluate the full picture, not just the number.

If credit is below your comfort level but the applicant has a solid explanation and verifiable income, consider approving them with an increased security deposit.

2. Income

The minimum income requirement is 2.5 times the monthly rent, with an ideal range of 3 to 3.5 times the monthly rent. For example, if rent is $1,200 per month, the tenant should earn at least $3,000 per month.

How to verify income:

- Pay stubs from the last two to three months.
- Bank statements.
- Tax returns for self-employed applicants.
- An offer letter for applicants starting a new job.

3. Criminal Background

Run a full background check on every adult applicant. Hard disqualifiers include violent crimes, sex offenses, arson, and major theft. Other offenses such as old misdemeanors or minor infractions should be evaluated on a case-by-case basis.

4. Eviction History

Run an eviction records search. Multiple evictions are a hard disqualifier. A single eviction from five or more years ago with a clear explanation may be considered on a case-by-case basis.

Red flags that threaten cash flow:

- Refuses to fill out the application completely.
- Provides fake pay stubs or fabricated references.
- Pressures you to skip the screening process.
- Cannot explain gaps in rental history.
- Multiple recent addresses, meaning they have moved every six months or less.
- Shows up late or not at all to the showing.

The Application Process
Step 1: Pre-qualify on the phone

Before showing the property, ask the basics: What is your monthly income? Do you have any pets? When do you need to move in? Have you ever been evicted? If the applicant does not meet your basic criteria, do not waste time showing the property.

Step 2: Show the property

Be professional and friendly. Point out key features, answer questions honestly, and provide an application to anyone who expresses interest.

Step 3: Collect the application and screening fee

Charge a screening fee per adult applicant to cover the cost of the background and credit checks, as well as your time reviewing the information. Get a signed application with authorization to run the background check, and collect employment information, rental history, references, and a Social Security number.

Step 4: Run screening

- Credit report.
- Criminal background check.
- Eviction history.
- Verify employment.

Step 5: Make a decision

If they pass, offer the property, sign the lease, and collect the deposit and first month's rent. If they do not pass, send a denial letter in compliance with the Fair Credit Reporting Act.

Legal note: You must apply the same criteria to every applicant without exception. Fair Housing laws are strict, and violations are costly.

Rent Collection Systems That Protect Cash Flow

Late rent is the number one cash flow killer and directly threatens your path to freedom. Set up a collection system from day one.

Options for Collecting Rent

1. Online Portals, the best option for consistent cash flow

Platforms such as Apartments.com, PayRent, TenantCloud, and TurboTenant offer automated payment processing, online rent collection, automatic late fee calculation, and complete records of every transaction. The main drawback is that some platforms charge tenants a processing fee, which they may complain about.

2. Zelle, Venmo, or PayPal

These are free and instant, and most tenants already use them. The downside is that they are not designed for landlords, lack automatic late fee enforcement, and become harder to track as your portfolio grows.

3. Checks

Simple and traditional, but tenants forget to mail them, checks bounce, and the process requires deposit trips and manual tracking. Not ideal for protecting cash flow.

4. Cash

Do not accept cash. It creates disputes about whether rent was paid, provides no paper trail, and generates cash flow headaches that are entirely avoidable.

Setting Rent Collection Rules

Put clear payment terms in your lease and enforce them consistently to protect your cash flow. Set a firm due date, a grace period if you choose to offer one, and a stated late fee structure. Charge a fee for bounced payments as well.

Be consistent. If you let a tenant slide once, they will expect it every time. Consistency protects cash flow and sets the professional tone for the landlord-tenant relationship.

Maintenance and Repair Systems

Maintenance calls will happen. Here is how to handle them efficiently without destroying your cash flow or your sanity.

The $100 Rule

- Under $100: Fix it immediately without overthinking it.

- $100 to $500: Get one or two quotes and approve quickly.

- Over $500: Get three quotes and evaluate your options.

Do not spend three hours researching how to save $30. Your time is worth more, especially as you build toward cash flow freedom.

Building Your Contractor Team

You need a reliable general handyman for small repairs, a plumber, an electrician, an HVAC technician, a roofer, a painter, and a lawn service if applicable. Find them by asking other landlords, joining local real estate investor groups, reading online reviews, and testing them on small jobs before trusting them with larger ones.

Pay your contractors quickly and treat them well. Good contractors protect your cash flow by keeping your properties rent-ready. When you find reliable ones, hold onto them.

Tenant-Caused Damage vs. Normal Wear and Tear

Normal wear and tear is your responsibility:

- Carpet wear from everyday living.
- Paint fading over time.
- Small nail holes.
- Worn faucet washers.

Tenant damage comes out of the security deposit:

- Holes in walls.
- Broken windows.
- Carpet stains.
- Appliances broken from misuse.

Document everything with photos before the tenant moves in and again after they move out. This protects your cash flow and the security deposit.

Dealing with Problem Tenants

You will eventually have a problem tenant. Here is how to handle it without letting it destroy your cash flow.

Late Rent. Cash Flow Killer Number One.

Day 4: Send a written late notice.

Day 10: Follow up with a call or text.

Day 15: File an eviction notice.

Day 30: Court hearing, judgment, and sheriff eviction.

Do not let late rent slide. Be kind but firm. Late rent becomes no rent. No rent destroys cash flow and delays your freedom.

Lease Violations

Common violations include unauthorized pets, additional occupants not on the lease, property damage, and disturbing neighbors. The process for handling them is the same in each case.

1. Document the violation in writing.

2. Send a written notice to cure, giving the tenant a specific number of days to correct the issue.

3. If the violation is not resolved, begin the eviction process.

The Nuclear Option. Eviction.

Evictions typically cost $400 to $1,500 and take 30 to 90 days depending on the state. They disrupt cash flow for months and should be avoided when possible through proper screening upfront.

When to evict:

- Non-payment of rent after 10 to 15 days with no resolution.

- Repeated lease violations.

- Illegal activity on the property.

- Property abandonment.

How to evict:

1. Serve the proper written notice, whether pay or quit, or cure or quit.

2. File an eviction lawsuit if the tenant does not comply.

3. Attend the court hearing.

4. Obtain a judgment.

5. The sheriff escorts them off the property.

Never do any of the following:

- Change locks while the tenant is still in the property.

- Turn off utilities.

- Remove their belongings.

- Threaten or harass the tenant.

Illegal eviction will cost you far more than following the proper process, and the resulting legal exposure will damage your cash flow even longer.

The Monthly Rhythm

Here is what managing a rental property actually looks like month to month.

Week 1:

- Collect rent, which is automated if you use an online system, securing your cash flow.

- Pay the mortgage.

- Review any maintenance requests.

Week 2:

- Follow up on any late rent to protect cash flow.
- Handle contractor appointments.
- Check on the property with a drive-by or a brief check-in with the tenant.

Week 3:

- Review expenses for the month.
- Update your spreadsheet tracking cash flow toward freedom.
- Plan for upcoming capital expenses.

Week 4:

- Address any outstanding issues.
- Plan for the following month.

Total time per property is typically 2 to 4 hours per month when things are running smoothly. Well-managed properties maintain consistent cash flow. Poorly managed properties bleed cash and delay freedom.

In the next chapter, we are talking about how to scale from one property to ten or more, using refinancing, equity, and leverage strategically to accelerate your path to cash flow freedom.

Chapter 10: Scaling from 1 to 10+ Properties

You have your first property. It is renting, cash flowing, and running smoothly. Now comes the question every investor asks: How do I get to 10 properties? How fast? And where does the money come from?

This chapter is your roadmap from one cash-flowing property to a portfolio that delivers cash flow freedom.

The Three Scaling Strategies

There are three ways to scale a rental portfolio.

1. **The Slow and Steady.** Buy one property per year using savings and income from your job.

2. **The Refinance Method.** Use equity from existing properties to fund new purchases.

3. **The Aggressive Approach.** Combine savings, refinancing, partnerships, and creative financing to buy two to three or more properties per year.

Strategy 1: The Slow and Steady. The Safest Path to Freedom.

This is the approach for most people building cash flow freedom.

How it works:

Year 1: Save $40,000, buy Property 1 at $300 per month cash flow.

Year 2: Save $40,000, buy Property 2 at $300 per month cash flow, for $600 per month total.

Year 3: Save $40,000, buy Property 3 at $300 per month cash flow, for $900 per month total.

Continue the same pattern each year.

Advantages:

- Low risk with no over-leveraging.
- Time to learn between purchases.
- Strong reserves maintained throughout.
- Steady, predictable progress toward cash flow freedom.

Disadvantages:

- Takes 10 to 15 years to build significant cash flow.
- Requires consistent savings discipline.
- Slower path to freedom.

Who this works for:

- W2 employees with steady income.
- Conservative investors.
- People starting in their 30s or 40s.
- Anyone who values security over speed.

Making It Work

If you are saving $40,000 per year for properties, here is how to get there.

Increase income:

- Salary increases of $5,000 per year add $417 per month.
- A side hustle adding $500 to $1,000 per month.
- Rental income from your first property at $300 per month.

Decrease expenses:

- House hack by living in a duplex and renting the other side.
- Cut lifestyle inflation.
- Delay major purchases.

Use tax refunds and bonuses:

- Do not spend your tax refund. Invest it directly into your property fund.
- Work bonus? Send it straight to the property fund.

The math:

$2,500 per month in savings times 12 months = $30,000

Plus $5,000 tax refund = $35,000

Plus $3,000 from first rental property cash flow = $38,000

That is enough to buy another property and add more cash flow toward freedom.

Strategy 2: The Refinance Method. Accelerating Cash Flow Freedom.

This is where real estate gets powerful for building cash flow freedom faster.

After three to five years of holding properties, you will have equity from appreciation, mortgage paydown, and any forced appreciation through renovations. You can tap that equity to buy more cash-flowing properties.

How Cash-Out Refinancing Works

Here is a realistic example. You bought a property five years ago.

Year 1:

Purchase price: $200,000

Down payment: $40,000

Loan amount: $160,000

Cash flow: $300 per month

Year 5:

Current value: $240,000 (from appreciation)

Loan balance: $151,000 (from paydown)

Equity: $89,000

Cash flow: Still $300 per month (rents rose, but so did some expenses)

Cash-out refinance at 75% LTV:

New loan amount: $240,000 × 75% = $180,000

Minus balance: $151,000

Cash out: $29,000

That is enough for a down payment on another cash-flowing property.

The key question is whether the property still cash flows after the refinance. If yes, you have just used existing equity to buy more cash flow toward freedom. If no, do not do it. Never sacrifice cash flow for growth.

The BRRRR Method. Buy, Rehab, Rent, Refinance, Repeat.

This is a popular strategy for scaling cash flow faster. Here is how it works.

1. **Buy a distressed property below market value.** Example: Purchase for $120,000 a property worth $160,000 after repairs.

2. **Rehab it to increase value.** Spend $20,000 on renovations for a total investment of $140,000.

3. **Rent it out.** The property rents for $1,400 per month and cash flows $300 per month.

4. **Refinance after 6 to 12 months.** Property appraises for $170,000. Refinance at 75% LTV

equals a $127,500 loan, pulling out most or all of your initial investment.

5. **Repeat.** Use that money to buy the next cash-flowing property.

The power of this method is that you recycle the same capital over and over, building cash flow streams faster.

The catch:

- Requires finding below-market deals.
- Requires managing renovations.
- Refinancing carries closing costs of $3,000 to $5,000.
- Only works if the property actually appraises at the expected value.
- The property must still cash flow after the refinance. This is non-negotiable.

Who this works for:

- Investors with renovation experience.
- Investors with access to distressed properties.
- Investors willing to put in sweat equity.
- Aggressive builders of cash flow freedom.

When Not to Refinance

Do not refinance in any of the following situations.

1. It kills your cash flow

If cash flow drops from $300 per month to $25 per month after refinancing, that is a bad trade. You are sacrificing monthly cash flow toward freedom in exchange for short-term growth capital.

2. Interest rates are significantly higher

If your current rate is 4.5 percent and new rates are 7 percent, refinancing destroys your numbers and your cash flow.

3. You do not have a plan for the money

Do not pull out equity just because you can. Only refinance to buy another cash-flowing property or make a strategic investment that increases your overall cash flow.

4. The property barely appraises

If there is not enough equity to make it worthwhile, meaning at least $30,000 in cash out, do not bother.

Strategy 3: The Aggressive Approach. Two to Three or More Properties Per Year.

This strategy is for investors who want to reach cash flow freedom as quickly as possible.

How to fund multiple purchases per year:

Source 1: W2 Income and Savings

Save aggressively at $50,000 to $60,000 per year by living well below your means, building side hustles generating $1,000 to $2,000 per month, house hacking to reduce or eliminate your housing costs, and maximizing income at your day job.

Source 2: Refinancing Existing Properties

As properties appreciate, pull equity every two to three years to fund new purchases that add more cash flow.

Source 3: Partnerships

Partner with other investors where you find deals and manage the properties and they provide the capital, splitting cash flow and equity 50/50. Two partnerships per year equals two more cash flow streams, even at 50 percent ownership.

Source 4: Seller Financing

Find motivated sellers who will finance part of the purchase. This reduces your down payment needs and lets you acquire more cash-flowing properties.

Source 5: Private Money Lenders

Borrow from individuals such as friends, family, or wealthy acquaintances at 6 to 8 percent interest for down payments. Pay them back when you refinance.

Example Aggressive Plan Toward Cash Flow Freedom

Year 1:

- Save $40,000 and buy Property 1, fully owned, at $300 per month.
- Total cash flow: $300 per month.

Year 2:

- Save $40,000 and buy Property 2, fully owned, at $350 per month.
- Partner on Property 3 at 50 percent ownership for $200 per month your share.
- Total cash flow: $850 per month.

Year 3:

- Refinance Property 1 and pull out $29,000.
- Save $30,000 for a combined total of $59,000.
- Buy Property 4 at $400 per month and Property 5 at $350 per month.
- Total cash flow: $1,900 per month.

Year 4:

- Refinance Property 2 and pull out equity.
- Partner on Property 6 at 50 percent ownership for $250 per month your share.
- Use private money for Property 7 at $400 per month.
- Total cash flow: $3,000 per month.

Result: $3,000 per month in cash flow within four years across seven properties, with five fully owned and two as partnerships.

Warning: This approach is aggressive and carries real risk. Only pursue it if you have strong cash reserves covering at least six months of expenses, you understand your markets well, you have systems in place, you can manage multiple projects simultaneously, you are using professional property management, and each property cash flows solidly.

Quality Over Quantity. Building Cash Flow Freedom, Not Bragging Rights.

The lesson from Chapter 2 bears repeating: Do not focus on the number of properties. Focus on cash flow per property.

Scenario A:

- Investor buys 12 properties in 5 years.
- Average cash flow: $150 per month each.
- Total monthly cash flow: $1,800.
- Time spent managing: 15 hours per month.
- Stress level: High.

Scenario B:

- Investor buys 6 properties in 5 years.
- Average cash flow: $400 per month each.
- Total monthly cash flow: $2,400.
- Time spent managing: 6 hours per month.
- Stress level: Low.

Scenario B wins every time. Higher cash flow, less work, and a faster path to freedom.

Focus on:

- Strong cash flow per property, with $300 or more per month as a minimum.
- Properties in growing markets.
- Quality tenants with low turnover and consistent cash flow.
- Solid property condition to keep maintenance costs low and cash flow protected.
- Properties you can afford to hold long term.

Do not chase:

- Property count for ego.
- Properties in declining markets just because they are cheap.
- Over-leveraged deals that barely cash flow.
- Properties you cannot afford to maintain.

Ask yourself with every deal: Does this property move me closer to cash flow freedom with solid monthly cash flow, or does it just add to my portfolio count? If it is the latter, pass.

How Fast Should You Grow?

Here is an honest recommendation for each stage of the journey.

Years 1 to 3: Go slow

Buy one to three properties. Learn the business. Make mistakes on a small scale. Build your first streams of cash flow.

Years 4 to 7: Moderate pace

Buy one to two properties per year. Refine your systems. Build your team. Accelerate cash flow growth.

Years 8 to 15: Scale strategically

Use refinancing and partnerships to acquire two to three properties per year when opportunities are strong. Your cash flow is compounding at this stage.

Years 15 and beyond: Maintain and optimize

Focus on paying down mortgages, increasing cash flow per property, and simplifying your portfolio. You are approaching or already in cash flow freedom.

The goal is not to own 100 properties. The goal is to own enough cash-flowing properties to replace your income and achieve cash flow freedom. For most people, that is 10 to 20 properties.

The Real Timeline. What Is Actually Achievable?

Conservative Timeline: One property every 18 to 24 months

- Year 5: 3 properties at $900 per month cash flow, which is 15 percent toward freedom if the target is $6,000.

- Year 10: 6 properties at $2,200 per month cash flow, which is 37 percent toward freedom as mortgages pay down.

- Year 15: 9 properties at $4,500 per month cash flow, which is 75 percent toward freedom.

- Year 20: 12 properties at $8,000 or more per month cash flow, which is 133 percent of the freedom number with several properties fully paid off.

Moderate Timeline: One property per year

- Year 5: 5 properties at $1,500 per month cash flow, which is 25 percent toward freedom.

- Year 10: 10 properties at $4,000 per month cash flow, which is 67 percent toward freedom.

- Year 15: 15 properties at $8,000 per month cash flow, which equals 133 percent of the freedom number.

- Year 20: 20 properties at $15,000 or more per month cash flow, with many properties paid off.

Aggressive Timeline: 1.5 to 2 properties per year

- Year 5: 8 properties at $2,400 per month cash flow, which is 40 percent toward freedom.

- Year 10: 15 properties at $6,000 per month cash flow, which equals 100 percent cash flow freedom.

- Year 15: 22 properties at $12,000 per month cash flow, which is 200 percent of the freedom number.

- Year 20: 30 properties at $25,000 or more per month cash flow.

All timelines assume you hold long term, properties appreciate at 3 percent annually, rents increase 2 to 3 percent annually, and you reinvest cash flow into reserves and new purchases.

The Compound Effect of Time on Cash Flow Freedom

Here is what most people miss. Your early properties become cash flow powerhouses over time. Consider what a single property purchased in Year 1 looks like as the years pass.

- Year 5: $300 per month cash flow, $40,000 in equity.

- Year 10: $450 per month cash flow, $95,000 in equity.

- Year 15: $650 per month cash flow, $175,000 in equity.

- Year 20: $1,100 per month cash flow, $280,000 in equity, or paid off entirely for pure cash flow.

That one property's cash flow more than triples over 20 years. Multiply that across 10 to 15 properties and you see exactly why buy-and-hold investing creates cash flow freedom.

Knowing When to Slow Down

There is a point where you should stop acquiring and start optimizing your cash flow.

Signs you should stop buying more properties:

- Your cash flow covers your living expenses comfortably, meaning you have reached freedom.

- You are stretched thin financially with no adequate reserves.

- You are stressed managing what you already have.

- You are buying just to hit a number rather than because the deal is genuinely strong.

- Your personal life is suffering as a result.

What to do instead:

- Pay down mortgages faster to accelerate cash flow.

- Improve existing properties to increase rents and net cash flow.

- Raise rents to current market rates.

- Refinance to a lower rate if available to increase cash flow.

- Enjoy the cash flow freedom you have built.

You do not earn bonus points for dying with 100 properties. The goal is cash flow freedom, not an empire.

Your Scaling Action Plan

Next 12 months:

- Buy Property 1 if you have not already.

- Set up systems for management.

- Build contractor relationships.

- Save for Property 2.

- Track your monthly cash flow toward your freedom number.

Years 2 to 3:

- Buy Properties 2 and 3.
- Refine your market selection.
- Track all expenses meticulously.
- Consider setting up an LLC or other legal structure.
- Celebrate hitting 10 to 20 percent of your freedom number.

Years 4 to 5:

- Evaluate refinancing options on early properties.
- Buy Properties 4 through 6.
- Hire property management if you have been self-managing.
- Build your team: CPA, attorney, and lenders.
- You are now at 30 to 50 percent of your freedom number.

Years 6 to 10:

- Continue acquiring one to two properties per year.
- Focus on cash flow optimization.
- Consider partnerships for larger deals.
- Reassess your freedom number; it may be closer than you think.
- Approaching 100 percent cash flow freedom.

Years 10 and beyond:

- Start paying off mortgages aggressively to accelerate cash flow.

- Transition from acquisition to optimization.

- Plan your exit from W2 work if desired.

- Enjoy the cash flow freedom you have built.

In the next chapter, we are talking about protecting everything you have built, including legal structures, insurance, and risk management that safeguards your path to cash flow freedom.

Chapter 11: Protecting Your Wealth

> *Disclaimer: I am not an attorney, and nothing in this chapter should be considered legal advice. The information provided here is for educational purposes only. Every investor's situation is unique, and the right legal structure for your portfolio depends on factors specific to you, including your state of residence, the number of properties you own, your financing arrangements, and your personal risk tolerance. Please consult a qualified real estate attorney to discuss your specific needs and options before making any decisions about entity formation or asset protection.*

You are building a real estate portfolio worth hundreds of thousands and eventually millions of dollars that generates cash flow toward your freedom.

One lawsuit, one uninsured disaster, or one major mistake could wipe it all out and destroy your path to freedom. This chapter is about protecting what you have built.

Legal Structures. Should You Use an LLC?

The most common question new investors ask is whether they should put their rental properties in an LLC. The short answer is yes, eventually, but probably not for your first property.

What an LLC Does

An LLC, or Limited Liability Company, creates a legal separation between you personally and your rental properties. If something goes wrong, such as a tenant suing you for an injury, a contractor filing a lien, or someone getting hurt on the property, the outcome depends entirely on whether you have that legal barrier in place.

With an LLC, they can only pursue assets held within that LLC, not your personal assets such as your home, vehicle, or savings. Your path to cash flow freedom is protected.

Without an LLC, they can pursue everything you own personally. Your entire journey to freedom is at risk.

When to Form an LLC

Property 1: Optional

Your risk is relatively low with a single property. Good landlord insurance can carry you through this stage. Focus on building cash flow first.

Properties 2 to 3: Strongly consider it

Once you have multiple properties, risk compounds. Your growing cash flow needs legal protection.

Property 4 and beyond: Absolutely do it

At this point you are running a real business generating significant cash flow. Legal protection is not optional.

How to Structure Multiple Properties

Option 1: One LLC per property

This provides maximum liability protection since one property's problem cannot affect the others or your total cash flow. It also makes selling individual properties easier. The downsides are higher setup costs of $100 to $500 per LLC, ongoing annual fees that vary by state, additional tax returns to file, and more administrative overhead.

Option 2: One LLC for all properties

This is simpler, cheaper, and easier to manage. The risk is that if the LLC is sued, every property inside it is exposed, which threatens your entire cash flow stream. Lenders may also require personal guarantees regardless of the LLC structure.

Option 3: Multiple LLCs grouping properties

Placing two to four properties per LLC balances protection with simplicity. This is a practical middle ground for most growing portfolios.

General ideas:

- Properties 1 to 3: Single-member LLC.
- Properties 4 to 10: Two to three LLCs, grouped by location or value.
- Properties 10 and beyond: Consult a real estate attorney for the optimal structure to protect your cash flow.

LLC Costs and Maintenance

Setup costs:

- DIY online: $100 to $300 per LLC.
- Attorney-assisted: $500 to $1,500 per LLC.

Annual costs:

- State filing fees: $0 to $800 per year, varying significantly by state.

- Registered agent: $50 to $300 per year.

- Tax return preparation: $150 to $500 per LLC.

States with low or no annual fees include Arizona, Missouri, Kentucky, and Colorado. States with high fees include California at $800 per year minimum, as well as New York and Massachusetts.

If you form an LLC, you must maintain it properly. This means keeping separate bank accounts, maintaining proper records, filing annual reports, and never commingling personal and business funds. If you fail to do this, courts can pierce the corporate veil and strip away the protection entirely, leaving your cash flow and personal assets fully exposed.

Financing with an LLC

Most residential lenders will not lend directly to an LLC. Your options are to buy the property in your personal name and transfer it to the LLC after closing, though some lenders prohibit this and you should review your mortgage documents carefully before doing so; to use commercial or portfolio lenders who lend to LLCs, which typically requires 25 to 30 percent down at higher rates that will impact cash flow; or to provide a personal guarantee, which means you are personally liable regardless and the LLC protection is limited in that context.

Talk to a real estate attorney and your lender about the best approach for your specific situation and cash flow goals.

Insurance. Your First Line of Defense for Cash Flow.

Before you even think about LLCs, get proper insurance. Insurance protects your cash flow from disasters.

Types of Insurance You Need

1. Landlord Insurance (Dwelling Policy)

This is not the same as homeowner's insurance and must be obtained separately.

What it covers:

- Property damage from fire, storm, and vandalism.
- Liability when someone is injured on the property.
- Loss of rental income if the property becomes uninhabitable, which directly protects your cash flow.

What it does not cover:

- The tenant's personal belongings, which require a separate renter's insurance policy.
- Flood damage, which requires a separate flood insurance policy.
- Earthquake damage, which requires a separate earthquake insurance policy.

Cost typically runs $800 to $2,500 per year depending on property value and location. Shop this annually, as rates vary dramatically between carriers. Saving $200 per year is $200 more in cash flow toward freedom.

2. Umbrella Policy

This provides extra liability coverage beyond your landlord policy, typically in the range of $1 million to $5 million, and costs only $200 to $500 per year. If someone sues you and wins a judgment larger than your landlord policy limits, the umbrella policy covers the gap. It protects your entire path to cash flow freedom from a single catastrophic lawsuit.

Example:

A tenant's guest slips on a wet sidewalk, is seriously injured, and sues for $2 million. Your landlord policy has a $300,000 liability limit. Without an umbrella policy, you are personally liable for the remaining $1.7 million, which destroys everything you have built. With a $2 million umbrella policy, the full judgment is covered and your cash flow freedom is protected.

Every investor with two or more properties should carry an umbrella policy. It protects all of your cash flow streams at minimal cost.

3. Flood Insurance (If Applicable)

If your property is in a flood zone, you must carry flood insurance separately. Standard landlord policies do not cover floods. Cost ranges from $400 to $2,000 or more per year depending on risk level. Check FEMA flood maps before purchasing any property. If it falls in a high-risk zone, factor this premium into your cash flow analysis before you buy.

4. Additional Coverage to Consider

- Rent guarantee insurance covers lost rent if a tenant does not pay, serving as an alternative to maintaining large reserves and directly protecting cash flow.

- Sewer line insurance covers expensive sewer repairs for $50 to $100 per year.

- Home warranty coverage for rentals covers appliance and system repairs for $400 to $600 per year.

Risk Management Beyond Insurance

Insurance protects you financially after something goes wrong. Preventing problems in the first place protects your cash flow even more effectively.

Tenant Screening. Your Best Cash Flow Protection.

This was covered in detail in Chapter 9, but it is worth restating here: 90 percent of landlord problems come from bad tenants. Bad tenants mean late rent, property damage, evictions, and destroyed cash flow, all of which delay your freedom. Spend the money on proper screening. It is the single best investment you will make to protect your cash flow.

Property Inspections

Inspect your properties on a regular schedule. If self-managing, visit quarterly. If using a property manager, require quarterly inspections with photos sent to you. If the tenant says there's no need to inspect, double down and get in there.

What to check:

- Major systems including HVAC, plumbing, and electrical.

- Safety items including smoke detectors, carbon monoxide detectors, and handrails.

- Maintenance concerns such as leaks, roof condition, and gutters.

- Tenant upkeep to confirm the property is being maintained properly.

Catching small problems early prevents them from becoming large and expensive problems that destroy cash flow.

Lease Agreements

Use a solid, state-specific lease agreement drafted by your state's landlord association or a real estate attorney. Do not write your own from scratch.

Key clauses that protect cash flow:

- Late fee policy.

- Maintenance responsibilities clearly assigned to each party.

- Guest and occupancy limits.

- Pet policy.

- Lease violations and available remedies.

- Renewal terms.

Have a real estate attorney review your lease at least once. Spending $300 to $500 now can save you $10,000 or more in litigation and lost cash flow later.

Documentation

Document everything that touches your property and your tenant relationships.

- Move-in photos and video.
- Move-out photos and video.
- All communications with tenants via email or text.
- All repairs and associated expenses.
- Lease violations.
- Full payment history.

If a dispute ends up in court, documentation is everything. It protects your cash flow, the security deposits, and your credibility.

Maintenance and Code Compliance

Stay ahead of routine maintenance to protect cash flow and avoid liability.

- Replace HVAC filters monthly.
- Service HVAC systems annually.
- Clean gutters twice a year.
- Test smoke and carbon monoxide detectors annually.
- Address tenant maintenance requests promptly.

Follow local codes:

- Occupancy limits.
- Lead paint disclosure for properties built before 1978.
- Smoke and carbon monoxide detector requirements.
- Handrail and general safety standards.
- Parking and unpermitted structures.

Code violations result in fines and personal liability if someone is injured. Both destroy cash flow.

Dealing with Major Disasters

Despite your best efforts, significant problems can occur that threaten your cash flow.

Property Damage from Fire, Flood, or Storm

If major damage occurs, take these steps immediately.

1. Ensure everyone is safe.
2. Document all damage with photos and video.
3. Call your insurance company immediately.
4. Secure the property by boarding windows or tarping the roof as needed.
5. Notify your tenant about next steps and timeline.

Insurance will typically cover repairs and rebuilding, lost rental income while the property is uninhabitable which protects your cash flow directly, and alternative housing for the tenant depending on your policy. You will be responsible for the deductible, which typically runs $1,000 to $5,000. Loss of rent coverage is what keeps your cash flow stream intact during the repair period. Confirm your policy includes it.

Lawsuits

If you are sued, call your insurance company immediately. They provide legal defense as part of your coverage. Do not speak directly with the plaintiff or their attorney; refer all contact to your insurance carrier. Document everything related to the incident and hire a real estate attorney if the matter is serious.

Most tenant lawsuits are frivolous and do not advance. Insurance handles them and protects your cash flow throughout the process.

Liens and Judgments

If a contractor or tenant obtains a judgment against you, they can file a lien on your property, potentially threatening your cash flow.

Prevention:

- Pay contractors promptly.
- Obtain lien waivers when making contractor payments.
- Follow all lease terms and applicable state laws.

If a lien is filed, work with a real estate attorney to resolve it, pay or settle the underlying debt, and file to have the lien released.

Tax Strategy and Cash Flow Protection

Work with a CPA who specializes in real estate investing. They will help you maximize depreciation deductions to keep more cash flow in your pocket, track deductible expenses properly, structure your entities correctly, plan for the tax implications of any future sales, use 1031 exchanges when appropriate, and optimize your overall tax strategy to protect and maximize cash flow.

A good real estate CPA typically costs $500 to $2,000 per year and returns thousands in annual tax savings. That is more cash flow working toward your freedom. Tax advantages are one of the four pillars of wealth, and a qualified CPA helps you capture every dollar of them.

Asset Protection Summary

Here is your complete protection checklist.

☐ Form LLCs for your properties once you have two to three.

☐ Get proper landlord insurance on every property.

☐ Get an umbrella liability policy with at least $1 to $2 million in coverage.

☐ Use solid, attorney-reviewed lease agreements.

☐ Screen tenants thoroughly to protect cash flow.

☐ Inspect properties on a regular schedule.

☐ Document everything.

☐ Maintain properties proactively.

☐ Work with a real estate CPA.

☐ Keep business and personal finances completely separate.

☐ Build cash reserves covering at least six months of expenses.

☐ Consult a real estate attorney about the right legal structure for your specific situation.

The goal is to build cash flow freedom and protect it.

In Part 4, we are shifting from building your portfolio to living off it, making the transition to cash flow freedom and designing the life you have been working toward.

PART 4: LIVING CASH FLOW FREEDOM

Chapter 12: Making the Transition

You have been building for years. You have 10, 15, maybe 20 properties. Your cash flow is strong. You are getting close.

The question everyone asks at this point: When do I actually have enough cash flow for freedom?

This chapter is about knowing when you have reached the finish line and what to do when you get there.

When You Have Enough

There is no magic number of properties. It is not about hitting 10 doors or 20 doors or 50 doors. You have cash flow freedom when your monthly property income comfortably exceeds your monthly expenses.

The Cash Flow Freedom Formula

Monthly rental cash flow must be greater than or equal to monthly expenses multiplied by 1.35.

The 1.35 multiplier gives you a buffer for major repairs, unexpected expenses, vacancies, lifestyle improvements, and peace of mind.

Example:

Your monthly expenses: $5,000

Your cash flow freedom number: $5,000 times 1.35 = $6,750 per month

If your properties generate $6,750 per month or more in cash flow, you have achieved cash flow freedom.

But Wait. What About...
What about inflation?

Rents rise with inflation. Your cash flow increases over time while your mortgage payments stay fixed or decrease as properties pay off. Inflation actually works in your favor when it comes to maintaining and growing cash flow freedom.

What about major expenses?

That is exactly what your reserves and the 1.35 buffer are designed to handle. Your cash flow freedom is protected.

What about market crashes?

You are holding long term. Markets recover. As long as you have reserves to weather six to twelve months of problems, your cash flow freedom survives and ultimately thrives.

What if I want to travel, buy things, or live better?

Then you need more cash flow. Calculate your desired lifestyle expenses and multiply by 1.35. That is your personal cash flow freedom number.

The Three Stages of Cash Flow Freedom

Stage 1: Expenses Covered

Cash flow equals your basic monthly expenses. You could leave your job, but life would be tight. You are at 100 percent of freedom.

Stage 2: Comfortable Freedom

Cash flow equals monthly expenses plus a 35 percent buffer. You can leave your job and live comfortably. This is true cash flow freedom.

Stage 3: Abundant Freedom

Cash flow equals 1.5 to 2 times your monthly expenses. You can leave your job, travel, give generously, and live abundantly.

Most people achieve cash flow freedom at Stage 2 and naturally progress to Stage 3 as mortgages pay down and rents increase.

The Psychology of Pulling the Trigger

Here is what happens when you get close to cash flow freedom: fear sets in.

"What if something goes wrong? What if I calculated wrong? Maybe I should wait one more year. Maybe I need two more properties."

This is normal. After decades of trading time for money, walking away from a paycheck feels terrifying, even when your cash flow says you are ready.

The One More Year Syndrome

Many investors keep working just one more year for five to ten years because they cannot bring themselves to step away. Do not let this be you.

Ask yourself honestly:

- Do the numbers work? Is my cash flow 135 percent of my expenses?

- Do I have 12 months of reserves in the bank?

- Are my properties stable with good tenants?

- Is my portfolio diversified across multiple properties?

- Am I working for security at this point, or because I actually need to?

If the numbers work and you have reserves, you have achieved cash flow freedom. You are ready.

The Soft Landing Approach

You do not have to go from full-time work to complete freedom overnight. Consider a gradual transition.

Year 1: Go part-time at your job, three to four days per week. Test your cash flow freedom while keeping some income cushion.

Year 2: Freelance or consult for 10 to 20 hours per week. Your cash flow covers most expenses and consulting covers the extras.

Year 3: Fully embrace freedom, or work only on passion projects.

This approach gives you a real test run of cash flow freedom while retaining some income as a cushion during the transition.

Shifting from Accumulation to Income Mode

Once you decide to embrace cash flow freedom, your entire strategy shifts.

Before Freedom. Growth Mode.

- Buying more properties.
- Building equity.
- Maximizing appreciation.
- Accepting some risk in exchange for growth.
- Building toward your cash flow freedom number.

After Freedom. Cash Flow Optimization Mode.

- Maximizing cash flow per property.
- Reducing debt to accelerate cash flow.
- Lowering risk across the portfolio.
- Simplifying the portfolio.
- Living your cash flow freedom.

Strategy 1: Pay Off Mortgages. Accelerate Your Cash Flow.

Once you are in cash flow freedom, start aggressively paying down mortgages. Paying off a mortgage is a guaranteed return equal to your interest rate. At 6 percent, paying it off early is a guaranteed 6 percent return with zero risk. It also dramatically increases monthly cash flow.

Which mortgages to pay off first?

- **Option A: Highest interest rate first.** This is the mathematically optimal approach.

- **Option B: Lowest balance first.** This creates psychological wins, simplifies faster, and delivers a quick cash flow boost.

- **Option C: Properties with the highest cash flow potential when paid off.** Target the properties where eliminating the mortgage will have the greatest impact on monthly cash flow.

Example:

Property A: $50,000 balance at 6 percent interest, currently cash flowing $200 per month.

Paid off: Cash flow jumps to $500 per month, a gain of $300 per month or $3,600 per year.

Property B: $80,000 balance at 5.5 percent interest, currently cash flowing $300 per month.

Paid off: Cash flow jumps to $700 per month, a gain of $400 per month or $4,800 per year.

Pay off Property A first. You reach the higher cash flow milestone faster and with less capital deployed. This is how you go from $6,000 per month to $12,000 per month in cash flow: pay off mortgages strategically.

Strategy 2: Sell Underperforming Properties

Not all properties in your portfolio will perform equally. Consider selling any property that cash flows under $200 per month, requires constant maintenance that eats into your freedom, sits in a declining neighborhood that threatens future cash flow, experiences high tenant turnover that disrupts cash flow, or simply demands more of your time and energy than it is worth.

Use a 1031 exchange to sell two to three underperforming properties, purchase one stronger property that cash flows more, simplify your portfolio, increase overall cash flow, and reduce the time you spend managing.

Example:

Before: Three properties generating $600 per month total at $200 each, with high maintenance demands, multiple tenants, and ongoing stress.

After (1031 exchange): One property generating $900 per month, single-family or small multifamily, simpler to manage, and more cash flow.

Same portfolio value. Better cash flow. A simpler life in freedom.

Strategy 3: Increase Rents to Market Rate

Many long-term landlords are undercharging because they have not raised rent in years. This leaves cash flow sitting on the table. Review your rents annually. If you are 10 to 20 percent below market, it is time to adjust.

How to raise rent without losing good tenants:

1. Give plenty of notice, ideally 60 to 90 days.

2. Explain that you are adjusting to market rate.

3. Make a small improvement before raising the rent, such as fresh paint or updated fixtures.

4. Increase gradually at $50 to $100 per month rather than a large jump all at once.

Example:

Ten properties currently renting at $1,200 per month.

Market rate: $1,350 per month.

Increase to $1,300 per month.

Additional cash flow: $1,000 per month, or $12,000 per year.

That is meaningful additional cash flow from properties you already own, strengthening your freedom without buying a single new property.

Strategy 4: Refinance to Lower Rates When Possible

If interest rates drop significantly below your current mortgage rates, refinancing can meaningfully increase cash flow.

Example:

Current mortgage: 7 percent interest at $900 per month payment.

Refinanced to: 5 percent interest at $750 per month payment.

Cash flow increase: $150 per month per property.

On 10 properties: $1,500 per month in additional cash flow, or $18,000 per year.

More cash flow means stronger freedom.

What Cash Flow Freedom Actually Looks Like

Let me paint you a realistic picture.

Year 1 of Cash Flow Freedom:

You wake up without an alarm. No meetings. No deadlines. No boss. You check your account and see $6,500 deposited from your rental properties. You spend four to six hours this month on property matters: approving a repair, reviewing property manager reports, and planning for an upcoming capital expense. The rest of your time is yours.

- Two-week travel without asking anyone for time off.
- Hobbies you set aside years ago.
- Time with family, free of financial stress.
- Passion projects with no financial pressure attached.

- Sleep, exercise, read, and whatever you choose.

This is cash flow freedom.

Year 5 of Cash Flow Freedom:

Two mortgages are now paid off. Cash flow has grown from $6,500 per month to $8,800 per month. You are more comfortable than when you first stepped away from work. Life is easier. Your freedom is stronger. You realize you worried for nothing.

Year 10 of Cash Flow Freedom:

Half your properties are paid off. Cash flow is $13,000 per month. You are living better than when you worked. You travel four to six months per year. You are helping your children with down payments on their first homes. You are writing checks to causes you care about. You own your time completely.

This is what you built this for. This is cash flow freedom.

Dealing with Freedom Challenges

Cash flow freedom is not without its adjustments. Here is an honest look at the challenges you may face.

Challenge 1: Boredom

Some people achieve cash flow freedom and realize that work gave them structure and a sense of purpose. If this happens, consider volunteering, starting a passion business with no financial pressure attached, mentoring other investors building toward freedom, joining boards or community organizations, taking classes, or building something meaningful outside of real estate.

Challenge 2: Healthcare

If you achieve cash flow freedom before age 65, you will
need to arrange health insurance coverage on your own.
Options include COBRA from your previous employer for
18 to 36 months, the Affordable Care Act marketplace,
private insurance plans, a healthshare plan, coverage
through a spouse's employer, or part-time work that
includes benefits. Costs typically run $500 to $1,500 per
month depending on coverage. Factor this into your cash
flow freedom budget from the start.

Challenge 3: Identity

For decades your identity was tied to your professional
title. When you achieve freedom, that structure disappears.
This is real and it takes time to adjust. Give yourself space
to settle into your new identity as someone who built cash
flow freedom and now owns their time fully.

Challenge 4: Social Pressure

Friends and family may not understand your decision. You
may hear: You are only 50, why are you not working? Don't
you get bored? Must be nice. Remember that most people
will never take the risks you took or make the sacrifices you
made to build cash flow freedom. You do not owe anyone
an explanation. Never apologize for what you have built.

The Cash Flow Freedom Decision Checklist

Before you step into full freedom, confirm these are in place.

    ☐ Monthly cash flow exceeds expenses by 35 percent or more.

    ☐ 12 months of reserves in the bank.

    ☐ All properties have stable, paying tenants.

    ☐ Property management in place or solid self-management systems established.

    ☐ Healthcare plan confirmed and budgeted.

    ☐ Spouse or partner is fully on board with the transition.

    ☐ Emergency plan in place for major expenses.

    ☐ Worst-case scenario numbers have been run and reviewed.

    ☐ You are mentally ready to leave your job.

    ☐ You have hobbies and activities to fill your time.

If you checked eight or more, you are ready for cash flow freedom.

In the next chapter, we are talking about what living the life you designed actually looks like and what comes next in your cash flow freedom.

Chapter 13: Living Your Cash Flow Freedom

You did it. You achieved cash flow freedom. Now what?

The First 90 Days

The first three months of cash flow freedom are an adjustment.

> **Month 1. Euphoria:** "I cannot believe I do not have to work. This cash flow freedom is amazing!"

> **Month 2. Disorientation:** "Wait. What do I do with all this time?"

> **Month 3. Settling In:** "Okay. I am finding my rhythm in freedom."

Give yourself grace during this transition. It takes time to adjust to cash flow freedom.

Managing Your Portfolio from Anywhere

One of the great benefits of rental property cash flow is that it is truly passive when you set it up correctly.

The Remote Landlord Lifestyle

If you are using a property manager, you can oversee your cash-flowing portfolio from virtually anywhere. Your monthly responsibilities typically look like this.

> Week 1: Review property manager reports to verify cash flow. About 30 minutes.

Week 2: Approve any repairs over $500. About 15 minutes.

Week 3: Review financials and cash flow for the month. About 30 minutes.

Week 4: Plan for upcoming capital expenses. About 30 minutes.

Total time: Approximately two hours per month.

You can handle all of this from your RV traveling the country, a beach abroad, a mountain cabin, or your couch. Technology makes it straightforward, with property management software such as AppFolio, Buildium, or TenantCloud; digital rent collection that automates cash flow; electronic lease signing; video inspections; and cloud-based accounting. Your cash flow arrives whether you are home or on the other side of the world.

The Seasonal Investor

Many people in cash flow freedom become snowbirds, spending November through March in Arizona, Florida, or abroad, and April through October in their home state.

For instance, I reside in Florida. We consider ourselves reverse snowbirds. We leave during the heat of summer to seek cooler climates to the north and west, then enjoy the rest of the year at home or traveling abroad.

As long as you have internet and a phone, your cash flow keeps coming. That is freedom.

Tax Strategies in Cash Flow Freedom

Your tax situation changes significantly when rental income becomes your primary source of cash flow.

How Rental Income Is Taxed

Rental income is taxed more favorably than W2 income, which directly protects your cash flow. There are four reasons for this.

1. Depreciation offsets a significant portion of your income, leaving more cash flow in your pocket.

2. Expenses are deductible, including property management, repairs, insurance, and travel to properties.

3. Rental income is not subject to FICA taxes, meaning no Social Security or Medicare withholding.

4. Passive loss deductions may apply depending on your situation.

Example:

Scenario A. W2 Employee:

Salary: $80,000

Federal tax: approximately $12,000

FICA: $6,120

Total taxes: $18,120

Take-home: $61,880

Scenario B. Cash Flow Freedom (Rental Income):

Gross rental income: $90,000

Depreciation: $30,000

Expenses: $25,000

Taxable income: $35,000

Federal tax: approximately $4,000

FICA: $0

Total taxes: $4,000

Take-home: $86,000

You are living on more cash flow and paying significantly less in taxes. That is freedom optimized.

Working with a Real Estate CPA

In cash flow freedom, a good CPA is one of the most valuable members of your team. They will help you maximize depreciation across all properties to protect cash flow, pursue cost segregation studies for accelerated depreciation that puts more cash flow in your hands now, plan for strategic property sales using 1031 exchanges to defer taxes, optimize entity structures, handle multi-state tax issues if you own properties out of state, and plan for estate and legacy considerations.

A good real estate CPA typically costs $1,500 to $3,000 per year and returns $5,000 to $15,000 or more in annual tax savings. Find one. Pay them. Listen to them. They protect your cash flow freedom.

Capital Expense Planning

Even in cash flow freedom, significant expenses will arise. Roofs run $8,000 to $15,000 every 20 to 25 years. HVAC replacements run $5,000 to $10,000 every 15 to 20 years. Water heaters run $1,000 to $2,000 every 10 to 15 years. Exterior and siding work runs $10,000 to $30,000 every 30 to 40 years.

The strategy is to maintain a capital expense fund that is completely separate from your operating cash flow. Set aside $200 to $300 per month per property into a dedicated savings account. When a roof or HVAC replacement is needed, you draw from that fund rather than your cash flow. This keeps your monthly cash flow stable, predictable, and undisturbed by major one-time expenses.

To Sell or Not to Sell?

At some point in cash flow freedom, you will ask whether it is time to start selling properties.

Reasons to sell:

- Simplify the portfolio by going from 15 properties to 8, with less to manage.

- Access a lump sum for a specific purpose.

- Unload a problem property that is consistently disrupting your freedom.

- Take advantage of peak market values.

Reasons not to sell:

- Capital gains taxes of 15 to 20 percent at the federal level plus state taxes.

- Loss of a cash flow stream that was generating income for you indefinitely.

- Depreciation recapture, which requires paying back a portion of the depreciation deductions you previously took.

The 1031 Exchange Option

If you do decide to sell, a 1031 exchange allows you to defer capital gains taxes by rolling the proceeds into another cash-flowing property. The process works as follows.

1. Sell the original property.

2. Within 45 days, identify one or more replacement properties.

3. Within 180 days, close on the replacement property.

4. Pay zero taxes on the gain at the time of sale. The tax obligation is deferred, not eliminated.

Strategy in cash flow freedom:

Sell three underperforming properties and exchange into one stronger property.

Before: Three properties generating $600 per month total at $200 each, with high maintenance demands, multiple tenants, and ongoing disruption to freedom.

After (1031 exchange): One property generating $900 per month, single-family or small multifamily, less management, and more consistent cash flow.

Same portfolio value. Better cash flow. Simpler freedom.

Leaving a Legacy

Eventually you will want to consider what happens to your cash-flowing properties after you are gone.

Estate Planning for Real Estate

Work with an estate attorney to address three core areas.

1. **Set up a trust.** A properly structured trust avoids probate, allows properties to transfer smoothly to heirs, and keeps the cash flow uninterrupted.

2. **Plan for taxes.** As of 2026, the estate tax exemption is approximately $15 million, though this is subject to change through future legislation.

3. **Decide on distribution.** You can leave properties directly to your children, who inherit at a stepped-up basis and avoid capital gains while inheriting the cash flow. You can sell and distribute cash. Or you can establish a trust that generates cash flow for heirs in perpetuity.

Passing Down the Cash Flow Freedom Strategy

The greatest legacy is not the properties themselves. It is teaching your children and heirs how to build cash flow freedom through real estate. Consider bringing adult children into the business to participate in property management and decision-making, gifting properties over time within annual gift tax exemption limits, creating a family LLC, and teaching them the buy-and-hold philosophy that created your freedom.

They will inherit properties that produce cash flow, the knowledge to manage them, the mindset that built the portfolio, and a clear path to their own cash flow freedom. That is generational wealth and generational freedom.

What Cash Flow Freedom Actually Looks Like

Imagine the life of these investors who achieved cash flow freedom through rental properties.

Dave, age 52:

Achieved freedom with 14 properties cash flowing $7,200 per month. Spends six months a year traveling in his RV with his wife. Manages properties from his laptop. Says the hardest part was adjusting to having nothing he was required to do.

Maria, age 48:

Achieved freedom with 11 properties generating $6,500 per month in cash flow. Started a nonprofit teaching financial literacy to underserved communities. Says she is busier now than when she worked, but it is work she loves. That is true freedom.

James, age 58:

Achieved freedom with 22 properties generating $14,000 per month in cash flow. Plays golf three times a week, volunteers at a local food bank, and is helping his children acquire their first rental properties. Says he wishes he had started earlier.

Linda, age 45:

Achieved freedom with 9 properties generating $5,800 per month in cash flow. Travels internationally six months per year, writes a travel blog, and works on photography. Says cash flow freedom is better than she imagined.

The common thread across all of them: none miss their jobs, and all say cash flow freedom was worth every sacrifice.

The Freedom You Have Earned

Here is what cash flow freedom actually means.

You wake up without an alarm. Not because you are unemployed, but because you do not have to be anywhere. Your cash flow arrives regardless.

You say yes to opportunities. A trip to Europe next month? Absolutely. Help a friend move? Of course. Last-minute concert? Why not?

You say no without guilt. Not today. Sorry, I cannot. Because I have cash flow freedom.

You are present. With your family. With your hobbies. With your life. You are not thinking about work deadlines during your child's game. You are not answering emails on vacation. You are not dreading Monday morning.

You own your life. That is cash flow freedom.

The Journey Was the Point

The properties are just tools. The cash flow is just money. The real prize is this - you proved to yourself that you could do it.

- You took risks when others played it safe.
- You delayed gratification when others lived paycheck to paycheck.
- You learned new skills when it would have been easier to quit.
- You built cash flow freedom that lasts.

The properties will eventually sell or pass to your heirs. But the person you became while building cash flow freedom? That belongs to you forever.

Your Next Chapter

Cash flow freedom is not the end. It is the beginning of the life you have been working toward.

So what will you do with your freedom?

- Travel the world.
- Start a business you are passionate about.
- Write a book.
- Volunteer full time.
- Spend time with grandchildren.
- Learn to paint, play guitar, or speak another language.
- Build something meaningful.
- Simply rest and enjoy.

The answer is entirely up to you. And that is the whole point of cash flow freedom.

📊 📊 📊 📊 📊 📊 📊 📊

Chapter 14: My Story

The information and formulas provided in this book are not just theories. They are real, they work, and I am living proof.

The Beginning

The year was 1999. I had previously worked a corporate job and hated every minute of it. I decided to make the jump to a real estate career. I imagined myself showing houses all day to pleasant people while touring beautifully decorated homes. Sounds lovely, does it not? The truth is, I had no idea what my future would hold.

A few months into my new career, I came face to face with a startling reality. As a fully commission-based sales professional, I had no retirement plan. Nothing. At twenty-four years old, I was on my own and had to figure it out.

My first instinct was to save as aggressively as possible, invest in the stock market or CDs, and hope for the best. For whatever reason, that approach did not sit well with me. I began looking around and asking a simple question: What did wealthy people do? What did they all have in common? The answer was real estate investments.

The First Property

I began my journey exactly the way I outlined it in this book. I started searching for properties and eventually found one: a completely vacant two-unit property. I located a private lender and borrowed the down payment from a family member. I was completely broke, with nothing in savings, but I found the money through others.

I bought the property.

My purchase price was $57,500.

It cash flowed by $400 a month.

Eight months later, I refinanced with a national lender for the amount I owed. No cash out. I simply wanted to pay off my private lenders and secure a lower interest rate, which reduced my monthly payment and increased my cash flow.

Three years later, I refinanced again and cashed out just over $40,000 in equity, which I used to purchase another property. Rents had increased, property values had risen, and my tenants had paid down a portion of my mortgage balance. Even after pulling out that much equity, the property still cash flowed $350 a month.

It was a thirty-year loan, but I made payments as though it were a fifteen-year loan.

Fifteen years later, that property was paid off. My cash flow exploded.

Lessons Learned Along the Way

My second property was a single-family home that cash flowed immediately. I sold it five years later to fund a business I was starting. I still regret that decision. In hindsight, I should have refinanced and pulled out the equity instead. That property would be paid off today, and my cash flow freedom number would be that much greater. Learn from my mistake.

The Snowball Effect

I purchased another property in my fourth year of investing, refinanced it after two years, pulled out cash, and kept moving toward my goal. Next came a small apartment complex, then a larger apartment complex, a triplex, duplexes, a commercial building, single-family homes, and the list continues to grow. The point is simple: you can do this. Start small, be patient, and eventually the snowball takes over.

Fast forward a couple of decades. I have always made it a priority to pay off mortgages within fifteen years or less. Why? Because it accelerates your cash flow freedom. It is, and always has been, what this is all about.

The Goal Becomes Reality

Years ago, I wrote out my goals, including the year I wanted to retire (aka leave the rat race) and the income I would need to do it. Rental properties were the vehicle to get there. I am happy to report that I exceeded that goal by more than 200 percent and shaved nearly ten years off my original timeline. And I am not finished. At the time of this writing, I just purchased another property and am in negotiations on yet another.

The Sacrifice Behind the Success

Was it always easy? No. I will not sugarcoat this for you. For years, we watched friends and family go on vacations, buy boats, get motorhomes, and purchase new cars. We did none of that. Not one bit. We chose to go without because we knew the end goal and we kept our eyes on it.

Life Today

Fast forward to today. I work when I want to. My husband and I travel six months out of the year. We have spent a month in Spain, a month in Italy, a month in Japan, and are preparing for a month in the Netherlands. We took a 3-month cross-country trip, allowing us to visit every state in the United States and most of the provinces of Canada.

I am living a life that most people only dream about. The social pressure along the way was real. The only people who truly understood our sacrifices were fellow investors who had also achieved cash flow freedom. When comments come from those around us, I remind myself of the work it took to get here. Nothing was handed to me. It was a lot of hard work. But was it worth it? Absolutely, yes.

Your Turn

The purpose of this book is to share the path to Cash Flow Freedom with you. This is not rocket science. Anyone can do it. With determination and a commitment to staying focused on the goal, you can find your own Cash Flow Freedom.

God Bless,

Cynthia

Conclusion: Your Cash Flow Freedom Starts Now

Let us come back to where we started.

You have spent most of your life trading time for money. Showing up. Clocking in. Building someone else's dream.

But now you know there is another way. Rental real estate. Cash flow freedom.

It is not glamorous. It is not quick. It is not easy. But it works.

The Path We Have Covered

You now know:

✓ How rental properties build wealth through four powerful forces, with cash flow as the foundation of freedom.

✓ The difference between being rich, affluent, and having cash flow freedom, and why cash flow matters more than property count.

✓ Your exact cash flow freedom number and how many properties it takes to get there.

✓ The buy-and-hold mindset that separates those who achieve cash flow freedom from those who stay on the hamster wheel.

✓ How to finance your first cash-flowing property, even with limited capital.

✓ How to find markets that cash flow and build long-term wealth.

✓ The numbers that actually matter for building cash flow.

✓ How to purchase your first property without making expensive mistakes.

✓ How to manage for maximum cash flow and minimum headaches.

✓ How to scale from one property to a portfolio that delivers cash flow freedom.

✓ How to protect everything you build with proper legal structures and insurance.

✓ When you have enough cash flow for freedom and how to make the transition.

✓ What living cash flow freedom actually looks like.

The Choice in Front of You

You have two paths.

Path 1: Do nothing.

Put this book down. Go back to your job. Keep trading time for money. Retire at 65, maybe. Hope it all works out. In 20 years, you will wonder what would have happened if you had started building cash flow when you had the chance.

Path 2: Take action.

Buy your first cash-flowing property in the next 6 to 12 months. Make mistakes. Learn. Adjust. Buy the next one.

Build your cash flow month by month. In 20 years, you will have cash flow freedom and wonder why you ever hesitated.

Your First Steps

If you are serious about cash flow freedom, here is what to do next.

This week:

☐ Calculate your cash flow freedom number as outlined in Chapter 3.

☐ Check your credit score.

☐ Open a spreadsheet to track your savings and future cash flow.

This month:

☐ Research cash-flowing markets as outlined in Chapter 6.

☐ Talk to two to three lenders and get pre-approved.

☐ Start looking at properties online.

☐ Join a local real estate investing group.

Next 6 months:

☐ Save your down payment and reserves.

☐ Analyze 20 to 30 properties to practice running cash flow numbers.

☐ Make offers on three to five properties.

☐ Buy your first cash-flowing rental property.

Next 2 to 3 years:

☐ Manage your first property and learn the business.

☐ Build systems and find reliable contractors.

☐ Save for Property 2.

☐ Buy Property 2 and increase your monthly cash flow.

Next 10 to 15 years:

☐ Continue buying one to two properties per year.

☐ Refine your strategy based on what is working.

☐ Build toward your cash flow freedom number.

☐ Make the transition to cash flow freedom.

The Only Guarantee

I cannot promise you won't have problems. You will have difficult tenants. You will have expensive repairs. You will have vacancies. You will have moments of doubt.

But here is what I can promise: If you buy cash-flowing properties in good markets, hold them long term, and manage them reasonably well, you will build cash flow freedom. Not might. Will.

The math is undeniable.
Time + Tenants = Cash Flow Freedom.

One Last Thing

Ten years from now, you will look back at today and think one of two things.

"I wish I had started building cash flow back then."

Or

"I am so glad I started building cash flow back then. I am free."

The only difference between those two futures is what you do next.

Your Cash Flow Freedom Starts Now

Not someday. Not when you have more money. Not when you feel ready. Now.

You have read the book. You have the blueprint. You know what to do. The only question left is: Will you do it?

I hope you will.

I hope that in 15 years you're writing to tell me how you achieved cash flow freedom and are living the life you always wanted.

I hope you prove to yourself that you are capable of more than you thought.

I hope you build cash flow freedom and own your time.

The path is clear. The choice is yours.

Let's build your cash flow freedom.

Appendix A: Deal Analysis Worksheet

PROPERTY ADDRESS: _______________________

PURCHASE ANALYSIS

Purchase Price: $_______________

Down Payment (___________ %):
$_______________

Loan Amount: $_______________

Interest Rate: _____________%

Loan Term: _____________ years

INCOME

Monthly Rent: $_______________

Other Income (laundry, parking, etc.):
$_______________

Gross Monthly Income:
$_______________

EXPENSES

Mortgage (P&I): $_______________

Property Taxes: $_______________

Insurance: $_______________

HOA (if applicable): $_______________

Property Management (8-10%):
$______________

Vacancy Reserve (7-10%): $______________________

Maintenance Reserve (10%):
$______________

CapEx Reserve (5-7%): $______________________

Total Monthly Expenses:
$______________

CASH FLOW ANALYSIS

Gross Income: $______________________

Total Expenses: $______________________

Monthly Cash Flow:
$______________

Annual Cash Flow: $______________________

RETURN METRICS

Cash-on-Cash Return: ______________%

Cap Rate: ______________%

DSCR: ______________________

1% Rule Check: ______________%

CASH FLOW FREEDOM IMPACT

My current monthly cash flow:
$______________

This property adds: $______________

New total monthly cash flow:
$______________

My cash flow freedom number:
$______________

Percentage toward freedom: ______________%

DECISION

☐ Buy. This property builds cash flow toward freedom.

☐ Pass. This property does not cash flow enough.

☐ Renegotiate.

Appendix B: Cash Flow Freedom Calculator

STEP 1: Calculate Your Monthly Expenses

Housing: $________________

Transportation: $________________

Food: $________________

Insurance: $________________

Debt: $________________

Kids: $________________

Lifestyle: $________________

Miscellaneous: $________________

STEP 2: Add a 35% Buffer

Total Monthly Expenses × 1.35 =
$________________ (Your Cash Flow Freedom
Number)

STEP 3: Calculate Properties Needed

Average cash flow per property:
$________________

Freedom Number ÷ Cash Flow Per Property =
________________ properties needed

STEP 4: Create Your Timeline

Current age: ________________

Target freedom age: ________________

Years to build: ________________

Properties per year needed: ________________

Appendix C: Resource List

Market Research

- Census.gov for population and demographic data.
- BLS.gov for employment data.
- Zillow.com for property values, rent estimates, and cash flow potential.
- Rentometer.com for rental rate comparisons.

Property Search

- Zillow, Realtor.com, and Redfin for listed properties.
- Local MLS access through a licensed agent.
- Auction sites such as Auction.com and Hubzu for distressed and foreclosure properties.

Financing

- Local banks and credit unions for portfolio and relationship-based lending.
- BiggerPockets lender directory for investor-friendly lenders.
- Online mortgage comparison tools for rate shopping such as Bankrate.com.

Property Management

- Local property management companies for full-service management.
- TurboTenant, TenantCloud, and Apartments.com as do-it-yourself tools for managing cash flow.

Legal and Financial

- A local real estate attorney for entity formation, lease review, and legal protection.

- A real estate CPA, best found through referral, to protect and optimize your cash flow.

- Insurance brokers who specialize in landlord and investment property coverage.

Education

- BiggerPockets forums and podcast for investor community and resources.

- The Real Estate Guys podcast for investing strategy and market insight.

- Local real estate investor meetups for networking and deal flow.

- State landlord associations for legal updates, lease templates, and landlord rights resources.

www.ingramcontent.com/pod-product-compliance
Lightning Source LLC
Chambersburg PA
CBHW071314150726
47997CB00002B/477